the life of Jesus

high school group study

jim burns

general editor

the life of Jesus

Published by Gospel Light
Ventura, California, U.S.A.
www.gospellight.com
Printed in the U.S.A.

Library of Congress Cataloging-in-Publication Data
Uncommon high school group study : the life of Jesus / Jim Burns, general editor.
p. cm.
ISBN 978-0-8307-4726-9 (trade paper)
1. Jesus Christ—Biography—Study and teaching. 2. Bible. N.T. Gospels—Criticism,
interpretation, etc. 3. Teenagers—Religious life. 4. Church work with teenagers.
5. Church group work. I. Burns, Jim, 1953-
BT301.3.U53 2009
232.9—dc22
[B]
2008040846

1 2 3 4 5 6 7 8 9 10 / 15 14 13 12 11 10 09 08

Rights for publishing this book outside the U.S.A. or in non-English languages are
administered by Gospel Light Worldwide, an international not-for-profit ministry.
For additional information, please visit www.glww.org, email info@glww.org, or write
to Gospel Light Worldwide, 1957 Eastman Avenue, Ventura, CA 93003, U.S.A.

dedication

To Dr. Mark Hughes:
Thank you, Mark, for your friendship.
Thank you for your fun and free spirit.
Thank you for your servant's heart.
Thank you for your support and encouragement
to the ministry of HomeWord and me.
Jesus was the Great Physician and Healer.
Thank you for following in His steps.

Jim Burns

contents

how to use the *uncommon* group bible studies

Each *Uncommon* Group Bible Study contains 12 sessions, which are divided into 3 stand-alone units of 4 sessions each. You may choose to teach all 12 sessions consecutively, to use just one unit or to present individual sessions. You know your group, so do what works best for you and your students.

This is your leader's guidebook for teaching your group. Electronic files (in PDF format) of each session's student handouts are available on *The Life of Jesus* DVD. The handouts include the "message," "dig," "apply," "reflect" and "meditation" sections of each study, formatted for easy printing. You may print as many copies as you need for your group.

Each session opens with a devotional meditation written for you, the youth leader. As hectic and trying as youth work is much of the time, it's important never to neglect your interior life. Use the devotions to refocus your heart and prepare yourself to share with kids the message that has already taken root in you. Each of the 12 sessions are divided into the following sections:

starter

Young people will stay in your youth group if they feel comfortable and make friends in the group. This section is designed for you and the students to get to know each other better. After the activity, you can show the introduction to the session from Jim Burns on the *Life of Jesus* DVD.

message
The message section will introduce the Scripture reading for the session and get students thinking about how the passage applies to their lives.

dig
Many young people are biblically illiterate. In this section, students will dig into the Word of God and will begin to interact on a personal level with the concepts.

apply
Young people need the opportunity to think through the issues at hand. This section will get students talking about the passage of Scripture and interacting on important issues.

reflect
The conclusion to the study will allow students to reflect on some of the issues presented in the study on a more personal level.

meditation
A closing Scripture for the students to read and reflect on.

unit I
the beginnings

When I started this project on the life of Christ, I had no idea of the great impact it would have on me personally. Writing and teaching these studies on the life and events of Jesus Christ is one of the most challenging and wonderful experiences in my Christian life. While once again studying some of the major events in the life of Jesus, I am reminded of the unconditional and sacrificial love of God.

I love the old Russian proverb that says, "He who has this disease called Jesus Christ will never be cured." I am convinced that if we seriously study the life of Jesus, we will never be the same. An encounter with Jesus Christ makes us different. Sometimes it makes us uncomfortable, revealing to us lives that have grown stagnant. At other times, it inspires us or gives us hope.

I once sat on the beach and watched a baby play in the sand. The little boy crawled around in the sand putting shells—along with anything else he could find—into his mouth. Eventually, he wiggled out of his already wet diaper and played the rest of the afternoon innocently. Like every child, he was so vulnerable and totally dependent on his parents' care. And then it hit me—God did that for me! God in the form of a vulnerable baby came into the world so that humankind would have the opportunity to live. He could have done it through marching armies or spectacular displays of miraculous power, but instead He chose to become a helpless little baby, humble and dependent on His own mother.

God's love is incredible. The all-powerful God of the universe became a baby to incarnate His life on earth. He was willing to follow the ritual of the day and be baptized by His cousin John. He was willing to withstand 40 days of temptation in order for the plan of redemption to eventually be accomplished. Studying the life of Christ is being aware of the insanely generous love of God.

My prayer for you and your students is that as you examine these incredible occurrences in the life of Jesus, you will catch a greater glimpse of the depth of His love and the strength of His commitment to you. My hope is that you will fall more in love with this God/Man who humbled Himself and then suffered and died so that we might be set free.

Make it your prayer that as you tell the stories of Jesus, the students in your group will not just intellectualize the life of Christ but also be inspired toward deeper commitments as they experience Jesus anew.

the birth of Jesus Christ

The people walking in darkness have seen a great light; on those living in the land of the shadow of death a light has dawned. For to us a child is born, to us a son is given, and the government will be on his shoulders. And he will be called Wonderful Counselor, Mighty God, Everlasting Father, Prince of Peace.

ISAIAH 9:2,6

Have you ever witnessed the wonderful and amazing process of a baby being born? Everyone who experiences the birth of a baby comes away with a new and refreshing perspective on life. Awe. Amazement. Tenderness. The miraculous birth of a child makes us different people.

So it is with the birth of Jesus Christ, the most miraculous birth of all. Jesus' coming into this world is surrounded by amazing miracles: His coming birth foretold hundreds of years before; the Holy Spirit coming upon a young, courageous teenager named

Mary; the amazing birth of His cousin John to a barren woman; the long journey of wise men following a bright and bold star; the startling, glorious appearance of thousands of singing angels praising God before a band of simple shepherds; the simple, humble, tender birth of the innocent Christ child.

The birth of Jesus Christ is a story that never gets old. It's a story that needs to be told and retold, experienced and lived in our hearts every day. Sure, everyone gets bombarded with the Yuletide Madison Avenue merchandising and materialistic media blitz, but nothing can dim or dampen the light of hope found in Jesus' coming to earth.

Although the students you work with may say they've heard the story a thousand times before, you can renew their fascination and appreciation for the birth of Christ by allowing the tenderness of His birth to touch your heart. Maybe it's time to teach this lesson in the maternity ward of a local hospital! Watching an innocent, newborn baby, your students will be amazed. Experiencing the new life found in Jesus Christ for themselves, your students will be transformed.

When we look at the manger we know how He loves us now, you and me, your family, and everybody's family with a tender love. And God loves us with a tender love. That is all that Jesus came to teach us, the tender love of God. "I have called you by your name, you are Mine."

MOTHER TERESA

the birth of Jesus Christ

starter

BIRTHDAY SCRAMBLER: Have all members of the group stand in a single-file line. Without any talking or writing, the group must organize themselves by birth date—month and day only. Give the group a set time to complete the task. After a few minutes, check the group's accuracy by having each person announce his or her birthday. Now insert the *Life of Jesus* DVD and watch session 1—an introduction to this study by Jim Burns.

message

The birth of Jesus is a mixture of grandeur and humility. The Son of God, the Savior of humankind, has come to the world. He has all power and all knowledge, but has come to spend time with us. Imagine that! Little ol' us.

At the same time, the King of kings and Lord of lords is born not to the highest-ranking couple in the land but to a lowly carpenter and his pregnant fiancée. And He doesn't come with the pomp and circumstance of a powerful king, but as a little baby, born in a barn surrounded by animals.

Why might Jesus have come to earth in such a quiet way? Why did He come as a baby when He could have come as a king?

_____

_____

_____

_____

_____

_____

_____

_____

_____

Before we dig into the story of Jesus' birth, there are two pieces of the pre-story that we have to understand: (1) prophecies about Jesus' birth, and (2) what is called the "virgin birth."

Jesus' birth foretold

There are many amazing aspects to Jesus' birth, but one of the most astounding is that people had predicted it hundreds of years earlier. The Old Testament has a number of prophecies (predictions of the future) about the events and circumstances surrounding the birth of the Messiah, Jesus Christ. These prophecies were given to people by God hundreds of years before the birth of Jesus—and, what's more, *they came true.* Let's look at two of these prophecies about Jesus' birth and how they were fulfilled.

1. Look up the following Old Testament Scripture concerning the place of the birth of the Messiah and describe what the prophecy was. Then read the corresponding New Testament passage to find out how it was fulfilled.

    Old Testament Prophecy—Micah 5:2

    _____

    _____

    _____

    _____

    _____

    New Testament Fulfillment—Matthew 2:1-6

    _____

    _____

    _____

    _____

    _____

2. How does King Herod use this prophecy?

    _____

    _____

    _____

    _____

    _____

    _____

    _____

    _____

3. Look up the following Old Testament Scripture concerning the manner in which the Messiah would be born and describe what the prophecy was. Then read the corresponding New Testament passage to find out how it was fulfilled.

Old Testament Prophecy—Isaiah 7:14

_____

_____

_____

_____

_____

New Testament Fulfillment—Matthew 1:18-23

_____

_____

_____

_____

_____

4. How are Mary and Joseph involved in the fulfillment of this prophecy?

_____

_____

_____

_____

the virgin birth

This second prophecy listed above begins to talk about another important aspect of this story: the virgin birth of Jesus. To refresh your memory, Mary and Joseph were engaged to be married. Then Mary received a visit from an angel who told her that she was going to become pregnant and give birth to God's Son, Jesus Christ. So she wasn't married yet; she was a virgin, and yet she was going to give birth to the Son of God. Here's Mary's account of this event from Luke 1:30-38:

> But the angel said to her, "Do not be afraid, Mary, you have found favor with God. You will be with child and give birth to a son, and you are to give him the name Jesus. He will be great and will be called the Son of the Most High. The Lord God will give him the throne of his father David, and he will reign over the house of Jacob forever; his kingdom will never end."
>
> "How will this be," Mary asked the angel, "since I am a virgin?"
>
> The angel answered, "The Holy Spirit will come upon you, and the power of the Most High will overshadow you. So the holy one to be born will be called the Son of God. Even Elizabeth your relative is going to have a child in her old age, and she who was said to be barren is in her sixth month. For nothing is impossible with God."
>
> "I am the Lord's servant," Mary answered. "May it be to me as you have said." Then the angel left her.

1. How does Mary react to the news of this incredible event?

   _____

   _____

   _____

   _____

2. What does this tell us about the kind of person Mary was?

_____

_____

_____

_____

_____

_____

_____

While Mary may have demonstrated incredible faith and calmness, her fiancé, Joseph, initially didn't take the news so well. Read Joseph's account in Matthew 1:18-25:

> This is how the birth of Jesus Christ came about: His mother Mary was pledged to be married to Joseph, but before they came together, she was found to be with child through the Holy Spirit. Because Joseph her husband was a righteous man and did not want to expose her to public disgrace, he had in mind to divorce her quietly.
>
> But after he had considered this, an angel of the Lord appeared to him in a dream and said, "Joseph son of David, do not be afraid to take Mary home as your wife, because what is conceived in her is from the Holy Spirit. She will give birth to a son, and you are to give him the name Jesus, because he will save his people from their sins."
>
> All this took place to fulfill what the Lord had said through the prophet: "The virgin will be with child and will give birth to a son, and they will call him Immanuel"—which means, "God with us."
>
> When Joseph woke up, he did what the angel of the Lord had commanded him and took Mary home as his wife. But he had no union with her until she gave birth to a son. And he gave him the name Jesus.

3. What was Joseph's initial reaction?

    _____

    _____

    _____

    _____

    _____

4. What made him change his mind?

    _____

    _____

    _____

    _____

    _____

5. What do we learn about the kind of person Joseph is in
    these passages?

    _____

    _____

    _____

    _____

    _____

    _____

dig

Now let's read through the story of Jesus' birth. The events of His
birth are told in two Gospels in the New Testament: Matthew

and Luke. We'll read the account of the birth of Jesus found in Luke 2:1-7. As you read, keep the following questions in mind: (1) Why were Joseph and Mary in Bethlehem? (2) What do you think Mary was thinking as she prepared to give birth?

> *In those days Caesar Augustus issued a decree that a census should be taken of the entire Roman world. (This was the first census that took place while Quirinius was governor of Syria.) And everyone went to his own town to register.*
>
> *So Joseph also went up from the town of Nazareth in Galilee to Judea, to Bethlehem the town of David, because he belonged to the house and line of David. He went there to register with Mary, who was pledged to be married to him and was expecting a child. While they were there, the time came for the baby to be born, and she gave birth to her firstborn, a son. She wrapped him in cloths and placed him in a manger, because there was no room for them in the inn (Luke 2:1-7).*

1. After you have read these verses, take a moment to write down any questions that you might have.

   _____

   _____

   _____

   _____

   _____

   _____

   _____

   _____

   _____

   _____

   _____

2. We can see God's hand in every aspect of Jesus' birth. The
    prophecies said that the Messiah would be born in the town
    of Bethlehem, but Joseph and Mary were from Nazareth.
    How did Joseph and Mary end up in Bethlehem?

    _____

    _____

    _____

    _____

    _____

    _____

3. Although conditions may have been more primitive than
    today, most babies in Jesus' day were not born in stables
    next to animals. If God planned this all out, why would
    He have had His Son born in such meager conditions?

    _____

    _____

    _____

    _____

    _____

    _____

    _____

Mary and Joseph get two sets of visitors after the birth of Jesus.
The first was a set of shepherds. Continue reading Luke 2:8-20 to
hear their story:

*And there were shepherds living out in the fields nearby, keeping
watch over their flocks at night. An angel of the Lord appeared to*

them, and the glory of the Lord shone around them, and they were terrified. But the angel said to them, "Do not be afraid. I bring you good news of great joy that will be for all the people. Today in the town of David a Savior has been born to you; he is Christ the Lord. This will be a sign to you: You will find a baby wrapped in cloths and lying in a manger."

Suddenly a great company of the heavenly host appeared with the angel, praising God and saying,

"Glory to God in the highest,
  and on earth peace to men on whom his favor rests."

When the angels had left them and gone into heaven, the shepherds said to one another, "Let's go to Bethlehem and see this thing that has happened, which the Lord has told us about."

So they hurried off and found Mary and Joseph, and the baby, who was lying in the manger. When they had seen him, they spread the word concerning what had been told them about this child, and all who heard it were amazed at what the shepherds said to them. But Mary treasured up all these things and pondered them in her heart. The shepherds returned, glorifying and praising God for all the things they had heard and seen, which were just as they had been told.

4. Angels appear to shepherds and tell them about the birth of Jesus. When the shepherds arrive, they find everything exactly as the angel had said. Why might the angel have appeared to a bunch of shepherds? Why not someone important or who had influence? (See verse 17 for help.)

_____

_____

_____

_____

_____

_____

_____

_____

The second visitors are referred to as the "Magi," the "Wise Men" or the "Three Kings." Now read the account of their visit as told in Matthew 2:1-12.

> *After Jesus was born in Bethlehem in Judea, during the time of King Herod, Magi from the east came to Jerusalem and asked, "Where is the one who has been born king of the Jews? We saw his star in the east and have come to worship him."*
>
> *When King Herod heard this he was disturbed, and all Jerusalem with him. When he had called together all the people's chief priests and teachers of the law, he asked them where the Christ was to be born. "In Bethlehem in Judea," they replied, "for this is what the prophet has written:*
>
> > *"But you, Bethlehem, in the land of Judah,*
> > *are by no means least among the rulers of Judah;*
> > *for out of you will come a ruler*
> > *who will be the shepherd of my people Israel."*
>
> *Then Herod called the Magi secretly and found out from them the exact time the star had appeared. He sent them to Bethlehem and said, "Go and make a careful search for the child. As soon as you find him, report to me, so that I too may go and worship him."*
>
> *After they had heard the king, they went on their way, and the star they had seen in the east went ahead of them until it stopped over the place where the child was. When they saw the star, they*

were overjoyed. On coming to the house, they saw the child with his mother Mary, and they bowed down and worshiped him. Then they opened their treasures and presented him with gifts of gold and of incense and of myrrh. And having been warned in a dream not to go back to Herod, they returned to their country by another route.

5. Why were the Magi in Bethlehem?

_____

_____

_____

_____

_____

_____

_____

6. How did the Magi respond to Jesus?

_____

_____

_____

_____

_____

_____

_____

_____

7. The response of the Magi is incredible because not only is Jesus just a little baby at this point, but also because the Magi were a part of another religion. In fact, of all the people God could have chosen, the first people He has visit Jesus are a group of shepherds and three guys from a dis-

tant land who were members of a different religion. Why do you think this is?

_____

_____

_____

_____

_____

_____

_____

apply

1. Think about Mary and Joseph. How would you respond if God asked you to do something incredible? If He nudged you to do something that maybe seemed crazy?

_____

_____

_____

_____

_____

2. Think about the Magi. They traveled days and days and hundreds of miles to see Jesus. They endured hardship and difficulties just to see this little baby. How hard are you seeking Jesus in your life?

_____

_____

_____

_____

3. Christmas has become more and more about the presents
    under the tree and less about the presence of Jesus. How
    do you and your family strive to keep Jesus the center of
    the Christmas season?

    _____

    _____

    _____

    _____

    _____

    _____

    _____

    _____

    _____

reflect

1. Read John 3:17. Why was Jesus born on this earth?

    _____

    _____

    _____

    _____

    _____

2. If Jesus knew His purpose, why would He have come as a
    little helpless baby? Why not just come down from heaven
    as a full-grown man?

    _____

    _____

_____

_____

_____

_____

_____

_____

3. What would have been the impact if Jesus' arrival had re-
    ceived more fanfare? Or if Jesus had been born to a promi-
    nent couple? Or if the angels had appeared to rulers and
    priests instead of shepherds?

_____

_____

_____

_____

_____

_____

_____

_____

meditation

But the angel said to them, "Do not be afraid.
I bring you good news of great joy that will be for
all people. Today in the town of David a Savior has
been born to you; he is Christ the Lord."

Luke 2:10-11

the incarnation
of God

He will stand and shepherd his flock in the strength
of the Lord, in the majesty of the name of the Lord his God.
And they will live securely, for then his greatness will reach
to the ends of the earth. And he will be their peace.

MICAH 5:4-5

Life is filled with astounding complexities and contradictory realities. For instance, if convenience stores are open 24 hours a day, 365 days a year, why do they have locks on the door? Why do teenage girls tend to go to the restroom in packs of four or five? How is it that some teenage guys spend more time on their hair than some girls? Why do the parents of teenagers set themselves up when they ask their sons or daughters, "What do you think I am . . . stupid?"

The incarnation of God in the person of Jesus Christ is one of the more complex and difficult concepts to explain to teenagers.

To begin with, it is a mystery. How could God become fully man and yet still remain fully God? To simplistically explain it off as a miracle that they must accept won't cut it for most teenagers. Teenagers want to investigate complex issues and discover God's truth on their own. In fact, this is something they need to do in order to personalize and internalize their faith. Because this world is already a complex place to begin with, the incarnation of God is a truth that can lead young people to explore their faith and seek God at a deeper, more meaningful level.

The simplest explanation of the incarnation is a changed life. A changed life is evidence to the truth of the incarnation's mystery. If Jesus Christ has invaded your life with His love and that love is poured out into the young people, the Incarnation will be a reality that they see in you. The abstract will be made concrete, just as the followers of Christ were amazed to see God at work in their presence.

That is why there is such power in building positive relationships with young people. Teenagers want love. They want hope. They want someone to trust. They want to believe and reach for someone greater than themselves—someone like God—but first they need to see that reality in someone's life—someone like you.

The incarnation of God is a wonderful mystery and miracle. The best explanation you can give to teenagers about the Incarnation is to allow Jesus to live His incredible life through you.

Whatever may happen, however seemingly inimical it may be to the world's going and those who preside over the world's affairs, the truth of the Incarnation remains intact and inviolate . . . Christ shows what life really is, and what our true destiny is.
MALCOLM MUGGERIDGE

the incarnation of God

starter

FULLY GOD, FULLY HUMAN: Christians believe that Jesus Christ is the incarnation of God. This means that although Jesus was fully a human man, He was also fully God. To explore this issue, complete the following exercise.

Christ

On the left, brainstorm which parts of Jesus represent His godliness. On the right, list which parts represent His humanness.

godly	human
(e.g., His resurrection)	*(e.g., His temptation)*
_____	_____
_____	_____
_____	_____
_____	_____

godly   human
(e.g., His resurrection)   *(e.g., His temptation)*

_____   _____
_____   _____
_____   _____

you

On the left, list areas of your own life where Christ is involved. On the right, list areas that still need to be given to Christ.

godly   human
(e.g., share Christ with my friends)   *(e.g., my relationship with Mom)*

_____   _____
_____   _____
_____   _____
_____   _____
_____   _____

our world

How does our world need us to be the incarnated love of God both in the spiritual realm and in the human realm?

godly   human
(e.g., pray for believers)   *(e.g., give to the needy)*

_____   _____
_____   _____
_____   _____

godly	human
(e.g., His resurrection)	*(e.g., His temptation)*

_____

_____

_____

_____

Now watch the introduction to session 2 on the *Life of Jesus* DVD.

message

Comprehending that Jesus was fully God and fully man at the same time is not an easy idea to grasp. It is easy to recognize that something can have multiple forms—like a caterpillar turning into a butterfly; or water being a solid, liquid or gas in its various states—but understanding that Jesus was simultaneously God and a human being is difficult to fathom.

In his Gospel, John provides us with one explanation of this dual-nature of Jesus Christ. As you read the following verses from John 1, keep the following questions in mind: (1) What does "the Word" symbolize? (2) What characteristics does "the Word" have?

> *In the beginning was the Word, and the Word was with God, and the Word was God. He was with God in the beginning.*
>
> *Through him all things were made; without him nothing was made that has been made. In him was life, and that life was the light of men. The light shines in the darkness, but the darkness has not understood it. . . .*

He was in the world, and though the world was made through him, the world did not recognize him. He came to that which was his own, but his own did not receive him. Yet to all who received him, to those who believed in his name, he gave the right to become children of God—children born not of natural descent, nor of human decision or a husband's will, but born of God.

The Word became flesh and made his dwelling among us. We have seen his glory, the glory of the One and Only, who came from the Father, full of grace and truth (John 1:1-5,10-14).

dig

1. Who is "the Word" in these verses? Why does John refer to Him this way?

_____

_____

_____

_____

_____

_____

_____

_____

2. What do we learn about Jesus from this passage?

_____

_____

_____

_____

_____

_____
_____
_____
_____

3. John 1:5 reads, "The light shines in the darkness, but the darkness has not understood it." What is this verse saying? Who or what is the darkness? Who or what is the light?

_____
_____
_____
_____
_____
_____
_____

4. Read Genesis 1:1 and John 1:1. Unlike Matthew or Luke, John does not begin his Gospel with an account of Jesus' birth, but rather with what sounds more like Genesis 1. Why do you think he does this?

_____
_____
_____
_____
_____
_____
_____

5. According to John 1:1-3, what part did Jesus, the Word, have
    in the creation of the world?

    _____

    _____

    _____

    _____

    _____

    _____

    _____

    _____

6. What does John 1:10-13 tell us about how Jesus was received
    into this world? What promise does it provide to those who
    choose to accept Him?

    _____

    _____

    _____

    _____

    _____

    _____

    _____

    _____

apply

Many people get confused when they try to figure out exactly who
Jesus really is. Is He God, or is He man? The answer is both! To
grasp this truth, we have to remember that our finite minds can-

not always comprehend an infinite God. Perhaps the best way to understand is to learn what the word "incarnation" means and how it is described in Scripture. The word "incarnation" literally means "embodied in the flesh." Jesus Christ was a man—an actual, physical man—but at the same time He was God in the flesh.

How was Jesus fully *man*? He was born of the flesh. Mary, His mother, physically gave birth to Him. There was a time and a place in which He was delivered into this world. He ate, slept and breathed, just like any other human being. However, the Bible also teaches that Jesus was fully *God*. From the beginning of time, He was in existence and was the creator of all things. He had the ability to know the secrets of the heart, to forgive sins, and to perform miraculous deeds.

Fully God, fully man.

1. Look up Colossians 1:15-20, Hebrews 4:14-15 and Philippians 2:5-8. List the godly and human attributes of Jesus described in these verses.

       godly   human

2. Hebrews 2:17 says, "For this reason he had to be made like his brother in every way." Why would the all-powerful, all-knowing King of kings and Lord of lords decide to come and deal with hunger, aching muscles, stress and B.O.? Why would Jesus do this?

_____

_____

_____

_____

_____

_____

_____

_____

_____

reflect

1. Each Christmas, we are reminded that God's gift to us is Jesus in the flesh. Your gift to God should be your very life. What areas of your life do you still need to give to God?

_____

_____

_____

_____

_____

_____

_____

_____

2. What comfort can you receive from knowing that Jesus has lived life as a human being?

_____

_____

_____

_____

_____

_____

_____

3. Why is understanding the incarnation an important part of seeing the big picture of the Christmas story?

_____

_____

_____

_____

_____

_____

4. When you think of Jesus, do you tend to think of His godly traits or His human traits? Why is it important to remember both aspects?

_____

_____

_____

_____

_____

_____

4. Look back at the list of godly vs. human areas of your own life that you made in the starter activity. Choose two items from your "human" list and write down some ways that you will work to give these areas over to God.

_____

_____

_____

_____

_____

_____

_____

_____

_____

_____

_____

meditation

For we do not have a high priest who is unable to sympathize with our weakness, but we have one who has been tempted in every way, just as we are—yet was without sin.

HEBREWS 4:15

the baptism
of Jesus

*A shoot will come up from the stump of Jesse; from his roots a
Branch will bear fruit. The Spirit of the Lord will rest on him—
the Spirit of wisdom and of understanding, the Spirit of counsel and
of power, the Spirit of knowledge and of the fear of the Lord.*

ISAIAH 11:1-2

I've always loved watching teenagers "go public" with their faith
through the ceremony of baptism. I've had the privilege of baptizing shivering young people as they waited in icy pools for their turn
to be "dunked for Jesus." Other students I've baptized have had it
easier—these fortunate teens were baptized in a warm, soothing
Jacuzzi. Whether it's watching teenagers sliding under the rushing
water of a frigid mountain stream at 6 o'clock in the morning or
standing on the ocean shore at 11 o'clock at night with flashlights,
baptism is a very special event in the life of every Christian.

The baptism of Jesus teaches all of us—youth workers and students alike—the importance of submitting to the will of God. When Jesus was baptized by John, He died to His will and completely submitted Himself to the will of His Father in heaven. Not only did He identify with the human traditions of His day, but He also defied human nature in its rebellion against God. In His baptism, Jesus stood with mankind in its need for redemption and stood against the power of sin by abandoning Himself to the power and will of God.

As a youth worker, you have the unique privilege of teaching young people the significance of Christ's baptism. You also can have the special opportunity to plan and prepare meaningful baptism ceremonies that they will remember forever. Baptism is a perfect opportunity for you to dig into your students' lives and encourage them to be all that God desires them to be.

Jesus doesn't ask you or your teens to do anything He wasn't first willing to do Himself. Jesus shows us that submitting ourselves to God is not only possible, but also that by submitting ourselves to God we receive the blessing of God.

Baptism is a celebration of new life. Only by submitting ourselves to God will we truly experience the celebration that He has planned for us.

Example is not the main thing in
influencing others. It is the only thing.
ALBERT SCHWEITZER

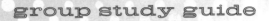

group study guide

the baptism
of Jesus

starter

BEEN BAPTIZED? Baptism is a beautiful symbol of new life in Christ and the washing away of sins. Have you ever been baptized? Have you ever seen someone else's baptism? Write down the different kinds of baptisms that you have seen.

_____

_____

_____

_____

_____

_____

_____

_____

_____

_____

_____

Once you have written these down, discuss the different types of elements and traditions with the members of your group. Then watch the introduction to session 3 on the *Life of Jesus* DVD.

message

Read the following account of Jesus' baptism from Matthew chapter 3. At this point, Jesus is an adult and has come to John the Baptist to be baptized by him. John the Baptist was born before Jesus and was used by God as a messenger to prepare the people's hearts and minds for the arrival of the Son of God.

As you read this passage, keep the following questions in mind: (1) How would Jesus' request to be baptized have made John feel? (2) How are the events depicted in this passage important in our understanding of Jesus as being fully God and fully man?

In those days John the Baptist came, preaching in the Desert of Judea and saying, "Repent, for the kingdom of heaven is near . . ."

John's clothes were made of camel's hair, and he had a leather belt around his waist. His food was locusts and wild honey. People went out to him from Jerusalem and all Judea and the whole region of the Jordan. Confessing their sins, they were baptized by him in the Jordan River.

But when he saw many of the Pharisees and Sadducees coming to where he was baptizing, he said to them: "You brood of vipers! Who warned you to flee from the coming wrath? . . . I baptize you with water for repentance. But after me will come one who is more powerful than I, whose sandals I am not fit to carry. He will baptize you with the Holy Spirit and with fire. His winnowing fork is in his hand, and he will clear his threshing floor, gathering his wheat into the barn and burning up the chaff with unquenchable fire."

Then Jesus came from Galilee to the Jordan to be baptized by John. But John tried to deter him, saying, "I need to be baptized by you, and do you come to me?"

Jesus replied, "Let it be so now; it is proper for us to do this to fulfill all righteousness." Then John consented.

As soon as Jesus was baptized, he went up out of the water. At that moment heaven was opened, and he saw the Spirit of God descending like a dove and lighting on him. And a voice from heaven said, "This is my Son, whom I love; with him I am well pleased" (Matthew 3:1-2,4-7,11-17).

dig

John the Baptist plays an important part in the life of Christ. He was even Jesus' relative by birth (see Luke 1:36). Let's learn a little bit more about John the Baptist by looking at some key aspects of his life.

1. Read Luke 1:5-20. Why was it hard for Zechariah to believe that his wife would bear a child?

    _____

    _____

    _____

    _____

    _____

    _____

    _____

2. What was the consequence of Zechariah's lack of faith?

_____

_____

_____

_____

_____

_____

_____

_____

_____

_____

3. According to the angel, what was John's role going to be?

_____

_____

_____

_____

_____

_____

_____

_____

_____

4. What similarities are there between this story and the story
    of the birth of Jesus?

_____

_____

_____

_____

_____

_____

_____

_____

_____

5. Now look at the passage we read in Matthew 3:1-6 again. What was John's message to the people?

_____

_____

_____

_____

_____

_____

_____

_____

6. How did John the Baptist fulfill the prophecy that was given in Isaiah 40:3?

_____

_____

_____

_____

_____

_____

_____

7. What do we learn in the Gospel accounts of John's appearance and style of living?

    _____

    _____

    _____

    _____

    _____

    _____

    _____

8. Why do you think the angel told Zechariah, "He is never to take wine or other fermented drink, and he will be filled with the Holy Spirit even from birth" (Luke 1:15)?

    _____

    _____

    _____

    _____

    _____

    _____

    _____

9. Read Mark 1:7-8. How does John say the baptism Jesus will perform will be different?

    After me will come one more _____ than I, the thongs of whose sandals I am not _____ to stoop down and untie. I baptize you with _____, but he will baptize you with the _____ _____.

apply

Imagine that you are a basketball player and one day Michael Jordan appears and asks you to shoot some hoops. Or that you're a huge fan of Aretha Franklin and one day she shows up and asks you to sing a duet. Or that you are a computer freak and one day Bill Gates arrives at your front door and asks to see your latest programming creation. Can you imagine what that would feel like?

This is similar to the situation in which John the Baptist found himself. John knew that his job was to prepare the people for the arrival of Jesus, the Son of God. He understood that he had an important role but that Jesus would offer the people something infinitely more valuable and eternal. Then, one day, Jesus walks up and asks John to baptize him.

Whoa.

1. Look up John 1:29-31. What do you think that John means when he says, "This is the one I meant when I said, 'A man who comes after me has surpassed me because he was before me'" (John 1:30)?

_____

_____

_____

_____

_____

_____

_____

_____

_____

2. Read Matthew 3:13-14. How did John respond when Jesus asked John to baptize Him? Why did he respond this way?

3. Read Matthew 3:16-17. What miraculous occurrences took place at the baptism of Jesus?

4. In session 2, we talked about the incarnation of God—that Jesus is both fully God and fully man. In light of this, why are the events of Jesus' baptism (especially verses 16 and 17) so significant?

_____

_____

_____

_____

_____

reflect

1. What does John the Baptist's life tell us about how God uses people for His purposes?

    _____

    _____

    _____

    _____

    _____

    _____

    _____

    _____

    _____

    _____

    _____

2. Most baptisms require a person to answer a set of questions or make a profession of faith. There are three key elements of this portion of baptism: (1) confession, (2) repentance, and (3) forgiveness. *Confession* involves understanding we have sinned and admitting our wrong doings. Read 1 John 1:9. What is the result of our confession?

    If we confess our sins, he is _____ and _____ and will _____ _____ _____ and _____ _____ _____ _____.

3. Why is confession important?

_____

_____

_____

_____

_____

_____

_____

_____

_____

4. What actions, thoughts and words do you need to confess
    to God?

_____

_____

_____

_____

_____

_____

_____

_____

_____

5. *Repentance* means feeling sorry for the wrongs that we
    have done and changing our thoughts and actions from
    our sinful ways. Read Acts 3:19. What does this verse say
    about repentance?

    Repent, then, and _____ _____ _____ , so that your sins
    may be _____ _____ , that times of _____
    may come from the Lord.

6. Look up the following verses. What does each reveal about how God views repentance?

    2 Peter 3:9:

    _____

    _____

    _____

    _____

    _____

    Luke 15:7:

    _____

    _____

    _____

    _____

7. Repentance involves turning away from our sins. What happens if you confess your sins but make no change in your future behavior?

    _____

    _____

    _____

    _____

    _____

    _____

    _____

    _____

    _____

    _____

8. In what areas of your life do you need to turn away from
   sin and turn back toward God?

   _____

   _____

   _____

   _____

   _____

   _____

   _____

   _____

9. *Forgiveness* is what God does when you faithfully and sin-
   cerely confess and repent. When you confess what you've
   done wrong and turn away from those thoughts and actions, God promises to cleanse you from your sin. Once
   you have confessed and repented for a sin, God forgives
   you completely and forgets it eternally. However, it is easy
   to hold on to feelings of guilt and remorse over past sins.
   Based on how God treats your forgiven sins, how should
   you act once you are forgiven?

   _____

   _____

   _____

   _____

   _____

   _____

   _____

   _____

10. Are there areas in your life where you have asked for and received God's forgiveness, but are not living as though your slate has been wiped clean? If so, in what areas?

_____

_____

_____

_____

_____

_____

_____

_____

_____

_____

11. Confession, repentance and forgiveness are necessary for us to practice in order to keep our relationships right with those around us. Describe a time when you used (or should have used) these three steps to make amends with a friend or family member.

_____

_____

_____

_____

_____

_____

_____

_____

_____

12. Baptism signifies a new life and a new beginning. What does Romans 6:1-4 say about the new life available in Christ?

_____

_____

_____

_____

_____

_____

_____

13. God chose Jesus' baptism to be the symbol of a tremendous change in Jesus' life—the beginning of His public ministry. Take some time to reflect on your own baptism. Do you view it as a significant event in your spiritual walk? What impact has it had on your life? On your faith?

_____

_____

_____

_____

_____

_____

_____

meditation

Therefore, if anyone is in Christ, he is a new creation;
the old has gone, the new has come!

2 CORINTHIANS 5:17

the temptation in the wilderness

Finally, be strong in the Lord and in his mighty power. Put on the full armor of God so that you can take your stand against the devil's schemes. For our struggle is not against flesh and blood, but against the rulers, against the authorities, against the powers of this dark world and against the spiritual forces of evil in the heavenly realms. Therefore put on the full armor of God, so that when the day of evil comes, you may be able to stand your ground, and after you have done everything, to stand.

EPHESIANS 6:10-13

Some of the most paralyzing accusations that Satan can throw at you as a youth worker are, "How can you possibly call yourself a Christian youth worker when you struggle with such thoughts and temptations? How can you expect to help young people become like Christ when you think and do things that bring shame to the cause of Christ? Ha!"

As uncreative as it is, Satan's strategy to discourage and break you down is the same strategy he tried on Jesus. Satan has been there, done that. His lies can penetrate your heart and mind with half-truths, searing accusations and all-out lies. He will do anything to weaken your resolve to follow Jesus and minister to students in need of His grace.

I know his ploys all too well. As a minister to young people and their families, I could become completely overwhelmed if I focused on the failings, inadequacies, sins and temptations with which I struggle. For as much as I encourage young people to live radically for God and allow Him to change their lives, I am as quickly dismayed when I see such slow spiritual progress in certain areas of my own life. That's why I unashamedly admit my need for God and throw myself on the grace of Christ, allowing Him to be the author and defender of my faith. I am not accountable to Satan. Because of Jesus Christ's blood for my sins, I can humbly and gratefully stand with God as His child.

Temptation stinks. There's no other way to say it. Yet if you're discouraged by the temptations in your life, I'm sure the story of Jesus' temptation in the wilderness found in this lesson will give you the perspective you need. Perfection is Christ's work. Progressing in the process God has initiated in your life is your choice and your responsibility. God has called you to a Person and a process. It is the journey you are walking with Jesus every day. He has all the grace you need to stand against Satan's sneaky strategies.

Jesus knows how to whip Satan. He's been there, done that.

Temptations in the life of faith are not accidents, each temptation is part of a plan, a step in the progress of faith.
OSWALD CHAMBERS

group study guide

the temptation
in the wilderness

starter

TOP TEN TEMPTATIONS: What are the biggest temptations facing teenagers today? In pairs, brainstorm the top 10 temptations that you and your peers face. Share your list with the group.

1. _____
2. _____
3. _____
4. _____
5. _____
6. _____
7. _____
8. _____
9. _____
10. _____

Now watch the introduction to session 4 on the *Life of Jesus* DVD.

message

Do you struggle with jealousy toward friends who always have the latest stuff? Are you prone to anger? Do you often find yourself gossiping? Guess what? Jesus struggled, too. Jesus Christ was perfect and sinless, but He still faced temptation just as we do. Hebrews 4:15 says, "For we do not have a high priest who is unable to sympathize with our weakness, but we have one who has been tempted in every way, just as we are—yet was without sin."

However, Jesus' temptation was different from ours in one key respect: He always overcame it. And we can as well. Jesus does not promise that life will be easy for us as Christians or that we will be immune to pain, suffering or temptation, but what He does promise is that He will always provide us with the means to be victorious over temptation. Look up 1 Corinthians 10:13. What promise is found in this passage?

No temptation has seized you except what is _____ _____ _____. And God is faithful; he will not let you be tempted _____ _____ _____ _____ _____. But when you are tempted, he will also provide ___ ____ ____ so that you can _____ ____ under it.

Open your Bible to Matthew 4. Just after being baptized, Jesus withdraws to the desert, where He spends the next 40 days fasting and praying alone. In this moment of physical and mental hardship, the devil—just as he often does with us—tried to ensnare Jesus in his trap.

As you read this passage, keep the following questions in mind: (1) What do you notice about the kinds of things the devil tempts Jesus with? (2) How does Jesus respond to the temptations?

Then Jesus was led by the Spirit into the desert to be tempted by the devil. After fasting forty days and forty nights, he was hungry. The tempter came to him and said, "If you are the Son of God, tell these stones to become bread."

Jesus answered, "It is written: 'Man does not live on bread alone, but on every word that comes from the mouth of God.' "

Then the devil took him to the holy city and had him stand on the highest point of the temple. "If you are the Son of God," he said, "throw yourself down. For it is written: 'He will command his angels concerning you, and they will lift you up in their hands, so that you will not strike your foot against a stone.' "

Jesus answered him, "It is also written: 'Do not put the Lord your God to the test.' "

Again, the devil took him to a very high mountain and showed him all the kingdoms of the world and their splendor. "All this I will give you," he said, "if you will bow down and worship me."

Jesus said to him, "Away from me, Satan! For it is written: 'Worship the Lord your God, and serve him only.' "

Then the devil left him, and angels came and attended him (Matthew 4:1-11).

dig

1. What is Satan called in Matthew 4:3?

   _____

   _____

   _____

   _____

2. The biblical meaning of the word "tempt" is actually more
    closely related to the idea of being "tested." The wilderness
    temptation was a true test of Jesus' faith. As we investigate
    this story, we can find many insights that apply to our own
    lives regarding temptations and the testing of our faith.
    Why do you suppose Christ went immediately from His
    baptism to His 40-day experience in the wilderness?

    _____

    _____

    _____

    _____

    _____

    _____

    _____

    _____

    _____

    _____

3. What types of things does Satan tempt Jesus with?

    _____

    _____

    _____

    _____

    _____

    _____

    _____

    _____

    _____

    _____

4. Notice how Satan tailors his temptations to be specific to
    Jesus' weaknesses at that moment. How does Satan frame
    his temptations? What techniques does he use?

    _____

    _____

    _____

    _____

    _____

    _____

    _____

    _____

    _____

5. In each exchange Jesus had with Satan, Jesus responded
    with a quote from the book of Deuteronomy. We can get a
    better understanding of each temptation by looking at why
    Jesus quoted each particular passage. On the chart below,
    write out what the three different temptations were and
    how Jesus refuted each.

temptation	Jesus' response
1. _____	1. _____
_____	_____
_____	_____
2. _____	2. _____
_____	_____
_____	_____
3. _____	3. _____
_____	_____
_____	_____

apply

Most often, temptation does not motivate us to commit horrible crimes. Instead, it favors a more subtle method: compromise. Temptation asks us to make small compromises in what we believe, in what we know to be true, and in what we know is right.

In C. S. Lewis's *The Screwtape Letters*, Screwtape, a senior devil, writes to his nephew, a devil-in-training, about the ways of tempting. (Keep in mind that when "the Enemy" is referenced, they are referring to God.) Screwtape tells his young apprentice:

> You will say that these are very small sins; and doubtless, like all young tempters, you are anxious to be able to report spectacular wickedness. But do remember, the only thing that matters is the extent to which you separate the man from the Enemy. It does not matter how small the sins are provided that their cumulative effect is to edge the man away from the Light and out into the Nothing. Murder is no better than cards if cards can do the trick. Indeed the safest road to Hell is the gradual one—the gentle slope, soft underfoot, without sudden turnings, without milestones, without signposts.[1]

1. What does Screwtape say about the magnitude of the sin a person commits?

_____

_____

_____

_____

_____

_____

2. According to Screwtape, what is the ultimate purpose of
    temptation?

3. What advice does Screwtape provide to his nephew about
    the best way to get a person to sin against God?

4. Satan used these same techniques when he tempted Jesus. He tried to convince Jesus to compromise His fasting for a piece of bread and His eternal purpose for momentary selfish power. Jesus showed us that compromise is not obedience. In what areas of your life have you found it easy to fall into compromise?

_____

_____

_____

_____

_____

_____

_____

5. Relying on God's infinite power is the only way to truly win the battle over our temptations, but there are often things in our situation that we can change, avoid or replace to help keep us from falling prey to Satan's snares. It might mean avoiding certain stores or websites, not hanging out with a particular friend, or not listening to certain kinds of music. What can you do or change that will help you combat your temptations?

_____

_____

_____

_____

_____

_____

_____

_____

reflect

1. How does it make you feel to know that Christ was also tempted?

   _____

   _____

   _____

   _____

   _____

   _____

   _____

   _____

2. Have you ever put the Lord to a test? If so, what did you learn from the experience?

   _____

   _____

   _____

   _____

   _____

   _____

   _____

   _____

3. In thinking about this story of Jesus' temptation in Matthew, why is it valuable to memorize important passages from Scripture?

    _____

    _____

    _____

    _____

    _____

    _____

    _____

    _____

4. Memorizing Scripture will allow you to call on God's promises when you need them most. Jesus used Scripture to respond to Satan's temptations, and you can rely on God's Word when you are faced with trials. Do you have a favorite Scripture passage? What makes it your favorite passage?

    _____

    _____

    _____

    _____

    _____

    _____

    _____

5. The following is a list of Scriptures to help you win the fight against temptation. Circle the passages that best relate to the temptations that you are facing, and then share

with the members of your group why you chose each particular Scripture.

Delight yourself in the Lord and he will give you the desires of your heart (Psalm 37:4).

But you will receive power when the Holy Spirit comes on you; and you will be my witnesses in Jerusalem, and in all Judea and Samaria, and to the ends of the earth (Acts 1:8).

And we know that in all things God works for the good of those who love him, who have been called according to his purpose (Romans 8:28).

Being confident of this, that he who began a good work in you will carry it on to completion until the day of Christ Jesus (Philippians 1:6).

And my God will meet all your needs according to his glorious riches in Christ Jesus (Philippians 4:19).

If any of you lacks wisdom, he should ask God, who gives generously to all without finding fault, and it will be given to him (James 1:5).

meditation

Submit yourselves, then, to God. Resist the devil, and he will flee from you. Come near to God and he will come near to you.

JAMES 4:7-8

Note

1. C. S. Lewis, *The Screwtape Letters* (New York: Macmillan, 1976).

unit II
significant events

I almost feel that before we begin this next unit with our students, we should take off our shoes. These four sessions are like holy ground. They give us a glimpse of some of the core events in the life of Jesus. Each session is another key moment in the purpose and ministry of Jesus.

Can I be honest with you? These sessions weren't as fun for me as some of the other sessions I've gone through with teens. In fact, most of this study has been more theological in nature than what I usually cover with students. I almost kept wanting to apologize to them and say, "Next month I promise that we'll study sex, drugs and rock music." But then it hit me: In this section, I was placing truth into the lives of my students.

The world was looking for the Messiah to come with a spectacular display of power and authority. Instead, Jesus gathers together a ragtag band of followers. How pathetic! He shows up to His greatest event riding on an ass. How ridiculous! His last recorded dinner is in some stuffy upper room where He has a customary meal and actually washes His friends' feet. How boring! Then He is crucified like a common criminal. How humiliating! This is the mundane, not the miraculous. This isn't spectacular; it's, well . . . ordinary.

Yet Jesus has a habit of entering the ordinary and radically changing it forever. He takes what looks like an ordinary event and makes it an eternal demonstration of love. In these sessions, don't miss the extraordinary in the simple acts of the life of Jesus.

As you teach these sessions to your students, I hope you will have some fun. But more than that, I hope you will be encouraged that as you cover these next four events in the life of Jesus, you are giving your students meat instead of milkshakes. This is pure protein. No one can encounter these events of Jesus and walk away the same.

Thanks for your efforts in working with teens. It has eternal benefits. Just ask Jesus!

the gathering of Jesus' disciples

Whoever serves me must follow me; and where I am, my servant also will be. My Father will honor the one who serves me.

JOHN 12:26

If I were Jesus and had to pick a bunch of teenagers to follow me and then entrust them to carry my message to the whole world, there would be a number of types that I *wouldn't* pick. For instance, I wouldn't pick any teenager with a bad attitude. Who wants to hang around with a whiner or complainer? I certainly wouldn't choose a flaky or irresponsible teenager. How could I ever get anything done if I couldn't count on my followers? I wouldn't select a teenager who was chronically late for every event. He'd probably miss every miracle I'd ever perform. I also wouldn't pick any teenager who was a loud mouth or who couldn't keep a commitment. What's the use of having followers if they're going to embarrass me? And I definitely wouldn't pick any teenager who wasn't al-together dependable and consistent in every word and action.

But then again, I'm not Jesus.

I'm so grateful that Jesus picked a ragtag bunch of inconsis-tent, irresponsible, undependable fishermen, tax collectors and other undesirable characters to change this world. You and I would have probably fit in just fine. So would the teenagers we work with. Jesus always has a way of doing things backward, side-ways and upside down in comparison with the way this world usually operates.

This lesson is an exciting chance for both you and your stu-dents to rediscover God's incredible love and grace. Jesus calls us to follow Him precisely because we aren't perfect. Your students can experience God's grace and acceptance by understanding that Jesus calls them to follow Him regardless of their weak-nesses. By following Jesus, both you and your students can lead the empowered life God calls you to in Jesus Christ.

They were not theologians or political leaders—just ordinary men who
became extraordinary under the molding hand of the Master Potter:
That makes His selection of them the more wonderful.

J. OSWALD SANDERS

the gathering of Jesus' disciples

starter

MODERN-DAY DISCIPLES: Imagine Jesus has come back to earth to choose 12 modern-day disciples. He has asked your group to help Him by providing a list of "The Top 12 Disciples." Design a group of modern-day disciples, and be ready to explain why you would choose these men or women.

1. _____

2. _____

3. _____

4. _____

5. _____

6. _____

7. _____

8. _____

9. _____

10. _____

11. _____

12. _____

Now watch the introduction to session 5 on the *Life of Jesus* DVD.

message

After Jesus' baptism by John the Baptist and His temptation in the desert, he begins His ministry at around the age of 30. One of the first things He does is to call His disciples. Although many times the word "disciple" is used only in reference to the 12 disciples or apostles who were closest to Jesus, a disciple is anyone who learns from someone else and follows that individual's teachings.

Read the following passage in Matthew 4:18-22. As you read, keep the following questions in mind: (1) How did Jesus convince Peter, Andrew and the others to follow Him? (2) How do the future disciples respond to Jesus' call? (3) How would you respond?

As Jesus was walking beside the Sea of Galilee, he saw two brothers, Simon called Peter and his brother Andrew. They were casting a net into the lake, for they were fishermen. "Come, follow me," Jesus said, "and I will make you fishers of men." At once they left their nets and followed him. Going on from there, he saw two other brothers, James the son of Zebedee and his brother John. They were in a boat with their father Zebedee, preparing their nets. Jesus called them, and immediately they left the boat and their father and followed him (Matthew 4:18-22).

dig

1. What does Jesus mean when He says, "I will make you fishers of men" (v. 19)?

    _____

    _____

_____
_____
_____
_____
_____
_____
_____

2. It is important to realize that this wasn't the first time Jesus had met these men. He had probably developed a relationship with His disciples before He called them to follow Him. Still, all that Jesus said to Peter, Andrew, James and John was, "Follow me." No sales pitch, no long list of benefits, no persuading. A simple "follow me," and each of them dropped what they were doing and joined Jesus. What can we learn from the disciples' response?

_____
_____
_____
_____
_____
_____
_____
_____
_____

3. The phrase "follow me" was a known one in Jesus' day; it implied Jesus was calling each of these men to be permanent disciples. None of the men were under the impression

that Jesus was just asking them to walk with Him down the street. They all knew that He was asking them to walk with Him *for life*. To follow Jesus, they had to give up their professions, their homes and, at times, even their families. As a disciple of Jesus Christ, what does it mean to put God first in your life?

---

4. How did the disciples demonstrate that they were putting God first?

5. Each disciple was willing to leave his old life behind in or-
    der to follow Jesus. They were attracted to Jesus' call and be-
    lieved in His ministry. Read Luke 14:25-27. What is Jesus'
    message to those who wish to follow Him?

    _____

    _____

    _____

    _____

    _____

    _____

    _____

    _____

6. The disciples were from all walks of life—fishermen, tax
    collectors, political zealots and even some high-society
    people. Throughout the ministry of Christ, God seemed
    to use people who were very different from one another.
    Why might Jesus have chosen people from all walks of life
    to be a part of His closest followers? Why didn't He just
    choose a handful of priests or religious experts?

    _____

    _____

    _____

    _____

    _____

    _____

    _____

    _____

    _____

7. The things today that try to grab our attention are often flashy, fast-paced, sexy or loud. Jesus was none of these things. What do you think attracted the disciples to Jesus?

8. What initially attracted you to Jesus? What attracts you to Jesus today?

9. When you think about sharing your faith with others, how can you convey the message of Jesus to a world bombarded by fast, flashy messages?

_____

_____

_____

_____

_____

_____

_____

_____

_____

apply

1. How do you know if God is taking the lead in your life? (Ask yourself these questions: *How do I spend my time? How do I spend my money? How do I spend my energy? What occupies my thoughts?*)

_____

_____

_____

_____

_____

_____

_____

_____

2. God doesn't want to be first in your life just on Sunday morning or at weekly Bible studies. He wants to be first every minute of every day of every year. At times, we all have trouble keeping God as our first priority in life. What things, activities or people in your life do you find tend to bump Jesus out of that top position?

_____

_____

_____

_____

_____

_____

_____

_____

3. The difficult thing to understand is that these things that take up our time, energy and thoughts may be good things; they may even be great things like spending time with family or volunteering or participating in church activities. But, if these good things become a higher priority than giving ourselves to God, they aren't really good at all. What helps you (or what can you do) to keep God at the forefront?

_____

_____

_____

_____

_____

_____

_____

4. What has being a disciple of Jesus Christ cost you?

_____

_____

_____

_____

_____

_____

_____

5. What God-given gifts and talents do you have?

_____

_____

_____

_____

_____

_____

_____

6. As a disciple of Jesus Christ, how can you use your gifts and talents for His glory?

_____

_____

_____

_____

_____

_____

_____

7. Have you experienced Christ using your life, your story
    or your position to influence others in positive and life-
    changing directions? If so, in what ways?

    _____

    _____

    _____

    _____

    _____

    _____

8. In the same way that Jesus called Peter, Andrew and James,
    He is calling you today. What is *your* reply? What things
    hinder you from saying yes?

    _____

    _____

    _____

    _____

    _____

    _____

9. What are you willing to do in response to His call?

    _____

    _____

    _____

    _____

    _____

    _____

reflect

1. What might the disciples have been thinking after hearing Jesus' call to come and follow Him?

    _____

    _____

    _____

    _____

    _____

    _____

    _____

2. Would you have followed Him? Why or why not?

    _____

    _____

    _____

    _____

    _____

    _____

    _____

3. What causes people to follow Jesus?

    _____

    _____

    _____

    _____

    _____

    _____

    _____

4. What makes following Christ so difficult today?

5. The disciples had to give up various things in order to follow Jesus. Some gave up their jobs and positions in society, while others gave up their family and friends. If Jesus lived in the flesh today and called *you* to follow Him, what would be the hardest thing for you to give up for Jesus? Why?

6. Finish these sentences:

The first time I felt God's call to follow Him was . . . (If you've never sensed God's call to follow Him, share that as well.)

_____

_____

_____

_____

When it comes to putting God first in my life, I . . .

_____

_____

_____

_____

_____

_____

The hardest part about following God is . . .

_____

_____

_____

_____

_____

_____

One thing I can do to keep God at the forefront of my life is . .

_____

_____

_____

_____

_____

_____

7. Jesus' influence has reached far beyond His first disciples
    and continues today. What strikes you the most about Je-
    sus' impact on the world?

    _____

    _____

    _____

    _____

    _____

    _____

8. Our lives can be used to do great things through Christ.
    How does it feel to know that God can use your life to have
    a worldwide impact for His kingdom? How can you pre-
    pare for God to do great things through you?

    _____

    _____

    _____

    _____

    _____

    _____

    _____

meditation

A new command I give you: Love one another. As I have loved
you, so you must love one another. By this all men will know
that you are my disciples, if you love one another.

JOHN 13:34-35

the triumphal entry

Hear the word of the Lord, you rulers of Sodom; listen to the law of our God, you people of Gomorrah! When you spread out your hands in prayer, I will hide my eyes from you; even if you offer many prayers, I will not listen. Your hands are full of blood; wash and make yourselves clean. Take your evil deeds out of my sight! Stop doing wrong.

ISAIAH 1:10,15-16

Youth ministry, like life in general, is a unique and often wild mix of triumph and tragedy. As I look back on my years of youth ministry experience, I can vividly remember numerous triumphant highlights. Going on countless snow ski, water ski, rock climbing and mission trips with every sort of teenager imaginable. Praying with students to receive Christ into their hearts for the very first time. Endless one-on-one conversations with young people about what God was doing in their lives. Moments filled with hilarious laughter and spontaneous water fights during long, hot car rides. Times of singing quiet worship songs by warm candlelight.

When Jesus entered Jerusalem on a young colt and was received by thousands of eager and excited people praising His name, perhaps He reflected on the special memories He shared with His disciples. Like the time His disciples came rushing back and exclaimed how they had cast out demons in His name. Or the time when Peter, James and John saw Jesus radiating all of God's glory during His transfiguration. Or maybe the time when the disciples' nets were so full with fish that their heavy nets almost broke.

Jesus' triumphal entry into Jerusalem reminds us of the praise He deserves in our lives. Yes, there were plenty of setbacks, disappointments and discouraging times that Jesus and His disciples faced when people rejected His message. However, for those few quick moments when Jesus came into Jerusalem on that dusty road, He certainly received the true praise and honor He deserved.

Why not take some time to reflect on the triumphs God has given you in your ministry? Why not praise Jesus for the triumphs He has worked in your life? This lesson is a great opportunity for you and your students to deepen your commitments to reflect on and praise Jesus for His triumphant entry into your lives.

Jesus did not come to change Israel's politics. He came to change men's hearts. When He rode into Jerusalem, Jesus presented Himself as a humble king, not a violent conqueror.
WARREN WIERSBE

the triumphal entry

starter

THE GRAND ADDRESS: Entrances can be a big deal. Think of the arrival of a boxer into the ring, the president of the United States into a room, or a singer onto a stage. Imagine that Jesus is coming to your high school and a huge ceremony has been planned. You have been asked to write an introduction to read over the loud speakers announcing Jesus Christ to the crowd. What would you say about Jesus? Write your introduction below, and then take turns reading this introduction aloud in your best grandstand voice.

Now watch the introduction to session 6 on the *Life of Jesus* DVD.

message

From the time of His baptism, Jesus spent roughly three years in full-time ministry healing the sick, preaching the gospel and forgiving sins. But Jesus has a bigger purpose—one that His entire life was leading up to (see John 3:16).

In the prior chapters in Luke, Jesus has been trying to warn His disciples about the events to come, but few things can prepare them for what they will witness. Jesus makes His public entry into Jerusalem on a day that we now know as Palm Sunday. It was a day of victory and rejoicing. People in the crowd praised Jesus as He entered Jerusalem. But few realized that in less than a week, many of these same people would also watch Him die on the cross, executed alongside common criminals.

Read the story of Jesus' triumphal entry in Luke 19:28-40. As you read, keep the following questions in mind: (1) Many people expected Jesus to come as a brazen king and a political power. How does Jesus' arrival contradict this perception? (2) Given the fact that Jesus knew what would await Him in a few days time, what might He have been feeling as He entered Jerusalem amidst the celebration in His honor?

> *After Jesus had said this, he went on ahead, going up to Jerusalem. As he approached Bethphage and Bethany at the hill called the Mount of Olives, he sent two of his disciples, saying to them, "Go to the village ahead of you, and as you enter it, you will find a colt tied there, which no one has ever ridden. Untie it and bring it here. If anyone asks you, 'Why are you untying it?' tell him, 'The Lord needs it.'"*

Those who were sent ahead went and found it just as he had told them. As they were untying the colt, its owners asked them, "Why are you untying the colt?"

They replied, "The Lord needs it."

They brought it to Jesus, threw their cloaks on the colt and put Jesus on it. As he went along, people spread their cloaks on the road.

When he came near the place where the road goes down the Mount of Olives, the whole crowd of disciples began joyfully to praise God in loud voices for all the miracles they had seen:

"Blessed is the King who comes in the name of the Lord!"

"Peace in heaven and glory in the highest!"

Some of the Pharisees in the crowd said to Jesus, "Teacher, rebuke your disciples!"

"I tell you," he replied, "if they keep quiet, the stones will cry out" (Luke 19:28-40).

dig

1. Before Jesus was to go into Jerusalem to celebrate the Passover, He asked His disciples to go to the nearby village of Bethphage and get a donkey's colt for Him to ride into the city. What is the significance of Jesus riding on the colt into Jerusalem?

   _____

   _____

   _____

   _____

   _____

   _____

   _____

2. While it was common for important religious or political figures to be able to use the livestock of the local people, Jesus tells His disciples exactly where to find the donkey and how the interaction to obtain it will go. What insights does this provide?

_____

_____

_____

_____

_____

_____

_____

_____

_____

_____

3. Turn to Zechariah 9:9-10 and read one of the Old Testament prophecies about the coming of Jesus. Based on these verses, what kind of savior were the people expecting?

_____

_____

_____

_____

_____

_____

_____

_____

_____

_____

4. According to Matthew 21:8 and Mark 11:8, what did the crowds do when Jesus came riding into Jerusalem?

_____

_____

_____

_____

_____

_____

_____

_____

_____

5. Read Psalm 92:12-14 and Leviticus 23:40-41. What is the significance of the palm frond?

_____

_____

_____

_____

_____

_____

_____

_____

_____

6. For the Hebrew people, the palm was the symbol of beauty and righteousness. It signified the "king" and was always associated with rejoicing as well as triumph and victory. According to Matthew 21:9 and Mark 11:9-10, what did the crowds shout?

7. "Hosanna" means "save now!" and was the cry a people in distress addressed to their king or their God. What kind of "saving" were the people looking for or expecting?

8. What kind of saving was Jesus actually bringing to them?

_____

_____

_____

_____

_____

_____

_____

_____

_____

apply

1. What do you think Jesus was feeling as He entered Jerusalem and saw the multitudes singing His praises, given the fact that He knew a few days later many of these same individuals would be shouting, "Crucify him! Crucify him!" (Mark 15:13-14)?

_____

_____

_____

_____

_____

_____

_____

_____

_____

2. Many of the people expected Jesus to arrive as a political king and have a powerful military presence. Why were the people hoping that Jesus would come as a political savior?

_____

_____

_____

_____

_____

_____

_____

_____

_____

3. How would you respond if Jesus rode into your town today? Would you be out on the streets singing His praises or would you stay home, embarrassed or ashamed?

_____

_____

_____

_____

_____

_____

_____

_____

_____

_____

4. In Jesus' day, people threw their coats and palm fronds on the ground before Jesus as a sign of respect and worship. What would we lay down today as a sign of our utmost respect if Jesus were to arrive?

reflect

1. Is there anything in your life that competes with Jesus for first place that you need to symbolically lay down before Him as a sign of worship and praise?

2. The triumphal entry of Jesus was a key event in His life. It
    is unique because He allowed Himself to be worshiped and
    called "king." What similarities and differences does Jesus'
    arrival into Jerusalem have with His arrival into the world?

3. Finish these sentences:

    Today, I am thankful to God for . . .

    The last time I worshiped God was . . .

One way that I enjoy praising God is through . . .

_____

_____

_____

_____

_____

_____

Jesus is worthy to be called King and Lord because . . .

_____

_____

_____

_____

_____

meditation

Let everything that has breath praise the Lord.

PSALM 150:6

the last supper

*So if you faithfully obey the commands I am giving you today—to love the
Lord your God and to serve him with all your heart and with all your soul—
then I will send rain on your land in its season, both autumn and spring
rains, so that you may gather in your grain, new wine and oil.*

DEUTERONOMY 11:13-14

Meals have often been a perfect appetizer to help me get to the
main course of ministering to a student in need. When I know a
teenager who is having problems at home or with friends or who
has simply dropped out of sight, the easiest thing for me to do is
to give him or her a call and ask that teenager to go out for a
meal. I've never known any teenager to turn down a free meal!

Meals provide a comfortable environment for face-to-face,
heart-to-heart conversations. Not only does sharing a meal set
the table for significant conversation, but it is also a wonderful
time to develop community and a deeper sense of security and intimacy among friends. Meals have been a key tool of my ministry

experience. Almost every high school and college ministry team meeting I've ever had has either begun or ended with a meal—a time to be together . . . no agenda . . . just friends . . . laughing and sharing our lives together.

When Jesus sat with His friends at their final meal together, it was the culmination of many special meals that they had shared together. The Last Supper was Jesus' opportunity to affirm, encourage, pray for and remind His followers of everything He had taught them during the previous three years. It was Jesus' time to show His disciples how to celebrate His life, death and resurrection through the intimate meal of Communion.

The closeness that Jesus' disciples experienced with Him at the Last Supper is the same intimacy Jesus wants to share with you. The words of Jesus, particularly in John 13–16, are the words of love He wants to remind you of right now. Jesus calls you to share a meal with Him. It may be Communion, or it may simply be inviting His presence around your table tonight. The intimacy and closeness found with Jesus at the Last Supper is not some distant, ancient biblical event. The living Christ requests the honor of dining with you tonight.

He loves you with more than the love of friendship. . . . He has given you all, and He asks for all in return. The slightest reserve will grieve Him to the heart. He spared not Himself, and how can you spare yourself?
HANNAH WHITALL SMITH

the last supper

starter

IDEAL DINNER: In 2007, author Melanie Dunea asked 50 prominent chefs in her book *My Last Supper* the same set of questions about the food, setting and company each would request for their final meal. If you could plan your one ideal dinner, what would it be? What would you eat? Where would you want to be? Who would you want to join you? Let your stomach dream and write your response below.

_____

_____

_____

_____

_____

_____

_____

_____

_____

In this study, we will look at Jesus' final meal with His disciples. In this case, the food was memorable not for its taste and presentation but for the symbolism and significance it would hold for thousands of years to come. After you finish, watch the introduction to session 7 on the *Life of Jesus* DVD.

message

In the last study, we looked at Jesus' triumphant arrival into Jerusalem. He was coming into the holy city of Jerusalem in order to participate in the sacred Passover celebration, an annual Jewish celebration commemorating the Israelites' exodus from Egypt and their deliverance from slavery. But this Passover would be different, as it would be the last time Jesus would gather together with all of His disciples before His death.

Read through the events of The Last Supper in Matthew 26:17-29. As you read, consider the following questions: (1) What events does Jesus foretell in this passage? (2) What might Judas have been thinking at the end of the evening?

> *On the first day of the Feast of Unleavened Bread, the disciples came to Jesus and asked, "Where do you want us to make preparations for you to eat the Passover?" He replied, "Go into the city to a certain man and tell him, 'The Teacher says: My appointed time is near, I am going to celebrate the Passover with my disciples at your house.'" So the disciples did as Jesus had directed them and prepared the Passover.*
>
> *When evening came, Jesus was reclining at the table with the Twelve. And while they were eating, he said, "I tell you the truth, one of you will betray me."*

They were very sad and began to say to him one after the other, "Surely not I, Lord?"

Jesus replied, "The one who has dipped his hand into the bowl with me will betray me. The Son of Man will go just as it is written about him. But woe to that man who betrays the Son of Man! It would be better for him if he had not been born."

Then Judas, the one who would betray him, said, "Surely not I, Rabbi?"

Jesus answered, "Yes, it is you."

While they were eating, Jesus took bread, gave thanks and broke it, and gave it to his disciples, saying, "Take it and eat; this is my body." Then he took the cup, gave thanks and offered it to them, saying, "Drink from it, all of you. This is my blood of the covenant, which is poured out for many for the forgiveness of sins. I tell you, I will not drink of this fruit of the vine from now on until that day when I drink it anew with you in my Father's kingdom" (Matthew 26:17-29).

dig

1. Why is this event commonly called "The Last Supper"?

_____

_____

_____

_____

_____

_____

_____

_____

_____

2. Jesus was coming into Jerusalem in order to celebrate
    Passover. To gain a better understanding of what Chris-
    tians call Communion, or the Eucharist, we must under-
    stand a little of the Passover meal eaten at the Last Supper
    of Jesus before His crucifixion. Read Exodus 12 in order to
    grasp what the Passover celebration is all about. What
    tasks were the Israelites instructed to do with the lamb?

    _____

    _____

    _____

    _____

    _____

    _____

    _____

3. Passover is also referred to as "the Feast of Unleavened
    Bread," and in Exodus 12:15 we read that the Israelites were
    instructed to make bread without yeast for seven days.
    What is the symbolism of having bread without yeast?

    _____

    _____

    _____

    _____

    _____

    _____

4. How is the lamb used as a symbol in the Bible?

_____

_____

_____

_____

_____

_____

_____

_____

_____

_____

5. In the Old Testament, before God sent His Son, Jesus, to heal and forgive the world, people were commanded to uphold the Law of Moses in order to be right with God. We are often more familiar with (and would rather focus on) the God of the New Testament, a God who forgives us, a God with whom we have been made right through the sacrifice of Jesus Christ. But this is not the God we see in Exodus 12:29-30. What are the consequences suffered by those who are not right with God?

_____

_____

_____

_____

_____

_____

_____

_____

_____

6. Now reread Matthew 26:20-25. What does Jesus say about the person who will betray Him?

_____

_____

_____

_____

_____

_____

7. What do you think Judas was thinking?

_____

_____

_____

_____

_____

_____

8. What might the other disciples have been thinking?

_____

_____

_____

_____

_____

_____

_____

9. In order to gain perspective on Jesus' accusation of Judas, read Luke 22:1-6. What do we learn about Judas based on these verses?

    _____

    _____

    _____

    _____

    _____

    _____

    _____

10. Imagine that you are Judas—that you are plotting to betray a man you have followed and worshiped for the last 3 years for 30 silver coins. A few days before your plan is to come to fruition, the very man you are going to betray, Jesus Himself, confronts you directly and says, "You, Judas Iscariot, are going to betray me." Most people would imagine that their plans would have been foiled and would have canned the whole idea. Why did Judas go ahead with his plan of betrayal?

    _____

    _____

    _____

    _____

    _____

    _____

    _____

    _____

    _____

    _____

11. Finish the story by looking at the events that occurred
next in Matthew 26:47-50 and Matthew 27:3-5. How does
Judas ultimately feel about his decision to betray Jesus?

_____

_____

_____

_____

_____

_____

_____

_____

_____

apply

1. How were Jesus Christ's words, as recorded in Matthew
26:26-29, a prophecy of His death? What does this tell you
about Jesus?

_____

_____

_____

_____

_____

_____

_____

_____

_____

2. What is the significance of the bread? The wine?

    _____

    _____

    _____

    _____

    _____

    _____

    _____

3. Why did Jesus choose such common symbols as bread and
    wine? Why wouldn't He have chosen special or rare foods?

    _____

    _____

    _____

    _____

    _____

    _____

    _____

4. Why is Communion (or the Eucharist) as special today as
    it was almost 2,000 years ago?

    _____

    _____

    _____

    _____

    _____

    _____

    _____

5. With any recurring event, the practice of taking Communion can become a mindless tradition. How can you keep the celebration of Communion a sacred and significant part of your faith?

6. Does Communion hold a personal significance for you? Or has it merely become a mindless monthly ritual you participate in with little thought? Why or why not?

reflect

We remember many of the events of Jesus' life throughout the year, but the Last Supper is one that is recreated and celebrated most frequently by Christians all over the earth. Participating in Communion is an act of remembrance that Jesus Christ's body was broken for us. He died so that we might live. It also means remembering that His blood was shed for us so that our sins would be forgiven. We are righteous before God only because of the broken body and shed blood of Jesus Christ.

1. What is the benefit or significance of knowing that thousands of Christians all over the world share the practice of Communion with you?

_____

_____

_____

_____

_____

_____

2. Judas had been a supporter and follower of Jesus and yet was still led to betray Him. Are there ways in your own life in which you betray Jesus? If so, in what ways?

_____

_____

_____

_____

_____

_____

3. Jesus told His disciples that the bread and wine symbolized His body and blood. Why did Jesus specifically want His disciples to remember His death every time they took Communion (as opposed to focusing on the Resurrection)?

_____

_____

_____

_____

_____

_____

_____

_____

_____

_____

4. Did Jesus forgive Judas? Explain your answer.

_____

_____

_____

_____

_____

_____

_____

_____

_____

_____

_____

5. Communion is a time of reflection on what God has done
    for us and on His awesome demonstration of love. How
    has God demonstrated His goodness and love in your life?

    _____

    _____

    _____

    _____

    _____

    _____

    _____

    _____

6. Communion is a time of confession. When we stand in the
    presence of Christ, we must confess our sins and shortcom-
    ings. To confess our sins to God means to agree with Him
    that we miss the mark of His perfection and need Him to be
    our Savior. What sins do you need to confess to God today?

    _____

    _____

    _____

    _____

    _____

    _____

    _____

    _____

    _____

    _____

7. Communion is also a time of dedication. Whenever we are aware of the ultimate sacrifice of Christ's love, we are drawn to dedicate our lives to Him and to be reconciled to Him. What areas of your life do you need to rededicate to God?

_____

_____

_____

_____

_____

_____

8. Finally, Communion is a time of praise. We can praise and thank God for His unconditional love. Communion reminds us of His kindness and goodness to our sinful world. What things does God deserve praise for?

_____

_____

_____

_____

_____

_____

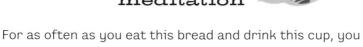

meditation

For as often as you eat this bread and drink this cup, you
proclaim the Lord's death till He comes.

1 CORINTHIANS 11:26, *NKJV*

the crucifixion of Jesus Christ

You see, at just the right time, when we were still powerless, Christ died
for the ungodly. Very rarely will anyone die for a righteous man, though for
a good man someone might possibly dare to die. But God demonstrates his
own love for us in this: While we were still sinners, Christ died for us.

ROMANS 5:6-8

As the son of a mortician, I grew up with death all around me. Yes, my dad was really a funeral director. Physically speaking, he was the guy who made sure you have an eternal resting place, whether that place was a hole in the ground or your ashes scattered over the Pacific Ocean.

I never really developed an appreciation for death (not that I was eager to experience it) until I became a Christian when I was 16 years old. Death never really had a strong impact on my life until I understood the significance of Christ's sacrificial death on the cross for me. When I did, I realized that without God, not only was I unprepared for eternal life but I was also headed for sure and certain eternal death.

My dad buried lots of people who died in all kinds of horrible and tragic ways. But he never buried anyone who had died through the torture and agony of crucifixion. Despite all the deaths I've heard about, nothing can compare to the injustice of the beating, whipping, mocking, spitting and crucifying of my Lord. What makes Christ's painful death even more unbelievable is the truth that He was completely innocent.

The sacrifice of Jesus displayed in His crucifixion is God's signature for His love for us. Death has been defeated by the power of God, and every blow that Jesus took was a blow against the sin of this world. The cross is not a symbol of death, but a sign of victory. Even a gruesome instrument of death designed to kill a King could not conquer the kingdom of God.

As you and your students reflect on the crucifixion of Christ in this lesson, remember that Christ's death was to free you from your death. In Christ, you are headed for sure and certain eternal life.

Even after generations of people had spit in his face, he still loved them. After a nation of chosen ones had stripped him naked and ripped his incarnated flesh, he still died for them. And even today, after billions have chosen to prostitute themselves before pimps of power, fame, and wealth, he still waits for them.

MAX LUCADO

the crucifixion of Jesus Christ

starter

FEAR OF DYING: Most people have a fear of dying in a particular manner (drowning, fire, animal attack, and so forth). What would be your least favorite way to go, and why?

_____

_____

_____

_____

_____

_____

_____

_____

_____

_____

Go around to the other students and share your answers. After you finish, watch the introduction to session 8 on the *Life of Jesus* DVD.

message

Crucifixion was the Roman method of execution for slaves and foreigners. Generally, it took a long time for a person to die on a cross, which made it excruciatingly painful. Death by crucifixion was unspeakably shameful and degrading. Yet Jesus Christ willingly suffered through the physical pain and humiliation of the cross in order to set humankind free from sin.

Matthew 27:27-44 can be a difficult passage to read, but it is an essential part of the story of our forgiveness and redemption. As you read this passage, keep the following questions in mind: (1) What might have been going through Jesus' mind as He endured these events? (2) Why didn't Jesus save Himself?

Then the governor's soldiers took Jesus into the Praetorium and gathered the whole company of soldiers around him. They stripped him and put a scarlet robe on him, and then twisted together a crown of thorns and set it on his head. They put a staff in his right hand and knelt in front of him and mocked him. "Hail, King of the Jews!" they said. They spit on him, and took the staff and struck him on the head again and again. After they had mocked him, they took off the robe and put his own clothes on him. Then they led him away to crucify him.

As they were going out, they met a man from Cyrene, named Simon, and they forced him to carry the cross. They came to a place called Golgotha (which means The Place of the Skull). There they offered Jesus wine to drink, mixed with gall; but after tasting it, he refused to drink it. When they had crucified him, they divided up his clothes by casting lots. And sitting down, they kept watch over him there. Above his head they placed the written charge against him: THIS IS JESUS, THE KING OF THE JEWS. *Two robbers were crucified with him, one on his right and one on his left. Those who passed by hurled insults at him, shaking their heads and saying, "You who are going to destroy the temple and build it in three days, save yourself! Come down from the cross, if you are the Son of God!"*

In the same way the chief priests, the teachers of the law and the elders mocked him. "He saved others," they said, "but he can't save himself! He's the king of Israel! Let him come down now from the cross, and we will believe in him. He trusts in God. Let God rescue him now if he wants him, for he said, 'I am the Son of God.'" In the same way the robbers who were crucified with him also heaped insults on him (Matthew 27:27-44).

dig

1. Read through the following different accounts of the Crucifixion in the three other Gospels. What new details or insights do you gain from reading these accounts?

   Mark 15:16-32

   _____

   _____

   _____

   _____

   _____

   _____

   _____

Luke 23:26-43

John 19:16-27

2. In Luke's account of the crucifixion (Luke 23:39-43), he
    includes a conversation between Jesus and the two crimi-
    nals crucified with Him. What two opinions do the crim-
    inals represent?

3. What do you think Jesus meant when He said, "Today you
    will be with me in paradise" (v. 43)?

    _____

    _____

    _____

    _____

    _____

    _____

    _____

    _____

    _____

4. Compare Matthew 27:35 and Psalm 22:16-18. Psalm 22 was
    written hundreds of years before the crucifixion of Jesus,
    yet it contains an amazingly detailed prophecy of what
    happened at the cross. What similarities do you find be-
    tween Psalm 22 and the crucifixion of Jesus?

    _____

    _____

    _____

    _____

    _____

    _____

    _____

    _____

    _____

    _____

5. What is the significance that hundreds of years before Jesus' death, the events of His crucifixion were foretold?

_____

_____

_____

_____

_____

_____

_____

_____

_____

_____

apply

1. Matthew 27:27-31 describes how Jesus was physically beaten and mocked before He was crucified. What do you imagine He was feeling—physically, emotionally and psychologically—during this ordeal of abuse?

_____

_____

_____

_____

_____

_____

_____

_____

2. What thoughts were perhaps going through the minds of Jesus' disciples?

    _____

    _____

    _____

    _____

    _____

    _____

    _____

3. What thoughts were perhaps going through the minds of those who had heard of Jesus but were not yet believers?

    _____

    _____

    _____

    _____

    _____

    _____

4. How would you feel if you were a disciple of Jesus and you had watched Him die on the cross?

    _____

    _____

    _____

    _____

    _____

    _____

    _____

reflect

1. Beyond Jesus' physical suffering, what else did He bear in His death?

_____

_____

_____

_____

_____

_____

_____

_____

_____

_____

2. Read 1 Peter 2:21-25. What lessons can we take from Jesus' crucifixion about how to handle adversity and struggles in our lives?

_____

_____

_____

_____

_____

_____

_____

_____

_____

_____

3. Why did Jesus stay on the cross?

_____

_____

_____

_____

_____

_____

_____

_____

_____

_____

_____

4. How would this story be different if Jesus did something
    that He could have done—take Himself off the cross? What
    would have been the impact on those at the crucifixion?
    What would have been the impact on us and our salvation?

_____

_____

_____

_____

_____

_____

_____

_____

_____

_____

_____

_____

5. What benefits have we received because of Jesus' death?

    _____

    _____

    _____

    _____

    _____

    _____

    _____

    _____

6. How does the knowledge of Christ's suffering on the cross
    help you to understand the depth of His love for you?

    _____

    _____

    _____

    _____

    _____

    _____

    _____

    _____

meditation

For we know that our old self was crucified with him so
that the body of sin might be done away with, that we
should no longer be slaves to sin—because anyone
who has died has been freed from sin.

ROMANS 6:6-7

unit III
sacrificial love

When I was a youth pastor at a large church in California, I got the shock of my ministry. One year right before Easter, I gave the students in our Sunday School class a pop quiz. The surprise came when most of the students flunked the test on the life and ministry of Jesus Christ.

Every week we sang about Him, we prayed to Him and the teens confessed their faith in Him as their Messiah. But in droves they couldn't communicate clearly the reasons for the birth, death and resurrection of their Lord. Few could even take a guess at what the Incarnation meant and, even though most had been baptized, many weren't sure of the biblical reasons for baptism. To be honest, I felt like a failure as a youth worker. If my students couldn't even talk intelligently about Jesus, was it worth it?

That Easter as we once again studied the wonderful fact that "Christ is risen, He has risen indeed!" I watched some of our students "get it." This section of the study isn't about the bloody, painful death of Jesus or even just about the facts surrounding the empty tomb. It's not about the incredible promise at the Ascension or the wonderful promise of His second coming. This section is about sacrificial love and redemption. It's about a price that was paid on a cross so that we might live abundantly and eternally. In the midst of the lessons, don't let the students miss the greatest love story that will ever be written. Jesus of Nazareth is our Savior, our Hope.

One of my favorite authors, Max Lucado, received a Christmas card with the following words that pretty much sum it up.

> If our greatest need had been information, God
> would have sent an educator.
> If our greatest need had been technology, God would
> have sent us a scientist.
> If our greatest need had been money, God would
> have sent us an economist. But since our greatest
> need was forgiveness, God sent us a Savior.

If you are anything like me, you may get discouraged at times because some of the students after all these years still do not completely understand the simple stories from the life of our Savior. But don't give up. There is someone in your group who has been waiting all his or her life for you to teach these wonderful stories, and this is the year that he or she will get it. And for all eternity, that person will thank you for being there for him or her.

the death of Christ

When he had received the drink, Jesus said, "It is finished."
With that, he bowed his head and gave up his spirit.

JOHN 19:30

For that one impossible student who ignores your every attempt to love him, Jesus cried, "It is finished." For the girl in your youth ministry with bulimia and a terrible self-image, Jesus cried, "It is finished." For the lonely, overweight boy with no social skills, Jesus cried, "It is finished." For the sweet, friendly girl who lives in an oppressive, legalistic, religious home, Jesus cried, "It is finished." For the ordinary teenager who struggles with gossip, impure thoughts and peer pressure, Jesus cried, "It is finished." For you, a sometimes tired and frustrated youth worker who wonders if your life is making a difference, Jesus cried, "It is finished."

It is finished.

That's all we really need to know. When Jesus said, "It is finished," it was finished. His death on the cross was the beginning of the end of every sin, frustration, tear, sadness, pain or trouble we experience. For every moment that you feel like you're making no progress with your students, Jesus' death can also put to death every thought of fear or worry you have.

Jesus' death is the turning point of all history . . . of your history. His death is the ultimate sign of love and sacrifice for this world's rebellion against God. Anything not hidden in the shadow of the cross stands exposed in the light of God. Because of the cross, you can bring every student before God and trust Him to finish His work in his or her life. You can also be assured that He is going to complete His work in you as well. Because of Jesus' sacrificial love, you can rejoice and agree with Him . . . *it is finished.*

People say they are tired of life; no man was ever tired of life; the truth is that we are tired of being half dead while we are alive. What we need is to be transfigured by the incoming of a great and new life.
Oswald Chambers

the death of Christ

starter

DARK TIMES: Think back to the darkest time in your life. What was one of your lowest points?

_____

_____

_____

_____

_____

_____

_____

_____

Recall the pain, anger, sadness and loneliness you felt during this time. Imagine that you had the ability to end all your pain and suffering, instantaneously, but instead chose to bear it for the sake of someone you loved deeply. You allowed yourself to suffer unbearable pain so that someone else didn't have to. Now, picture that this person whom you love so dearly and deeply doesn't understand why you are doing this or, even worse, doesn't appreciate your sacrifice. How would this make you feel?

_____

_____

_____

_____

_____

_____

_____

_____

_____

_____

_____

This is what Jesus experienced when He died on the cross. And though we may desire to hurry over the story of the death of Christ and get to the story of His glorious resurrection, in order to understand Jesus' sacrifice and God's immense love for us, we must first attempt to grasp the pain and suffering Jesus endured on our behalf.

This can be difficult. It is hard to imagine the emotional anguish that Jesus suffered, knowing that those He was dying for were laughing at Him and tormenting Him from below the cross. We cannot fathom what having the sin of the world on our shoulders would feel like to the soul. What we can attempt to understand, in some small way, is the physical pain that Jesus bore. While Jesus was fully God, He was also fully man, which means He suffered intense physical pain on our behalf. And why?

Because He loved us so much.

Take a moment to read through the following statement by Dr. Edward R. Bloomquist about the physical pain Jesus endured on the cross:

Like many others of His era, Jesus died on a cross by decree of Roman officials and endured one of man's most fierce tortures. But unlike others, He also bore the sins of the world on His sinless body—a spiritual agony we cannot begin to comprehend. We can, however, sense to a small degree His physical suffering.

Once in the tribunal area, the victim was stripped and his hands tied above his head to a supporting column. A soldier was stationed on each side of the condemned, and they took turns beating him with a flagrum—a short handle equipped with leather thongs whose ends were tipped with lead balls or sheep bones.

The thongs fell where they would, the leather strips burying themselves deep in the victim's body. When wrenched away, the lead balls ripped out bits of flesh. Hemorrhaging was intense, and the destruction of the condemned's body so extensive that even some Roman soldiers, hardened to brutality, were revolted.

National law prohibited more than 40 lashes. Ever cautious to uphold the law, Pharisees demanded the beatings be stopped at the 39th stroke. Rome had only one stipulation: The prisoner must remain alive and capable of carrying his crossbar to the execution.

Once the beating was completed, the near-naked victim was jerked to his feet, and the crossbar (weighing some 125 pounds) was laid on his shoulders. The condemned's arms were lashed to the crossbar, preventing a dash for freedom or striking out at his adversaries. A rope was commonly tied around his waist to direct his progress as he struggled through the streets. Romans preferred their victims naked; it was more humiliating. National preference, however, called for some clothing. The Romans usually agreed to this request by providing a loincloth.

Once the execution spot was reached, onlookers were held back and the victim was forced to the base of the stake. Then the crossbeam was removed from his back and experienced attendants threw him on the ground, grabbing his hands and stretching them out on the crossbar for size. The executioner placed an auger under each outstretched hand, and drilled a hole for the large crucifixion nail—a square spike about a third of an inch thick at its head.

The nail point was placed at the heel of the victim's hand. A single blow sent it ripping through the tissue, separating the carpal bones as it plunged into the crossbar. Paintings usually show the nail through the palm. Anatomically, this is impractical; the tissue cannot bear weight, and the victims would drop to the ground within minutes after being elevated.

Usually, the nail tore through the median nerve, creating an unending trail of fire up the victim's arms, augmenting the pain that tortured his body. From this moment on, this pain would intensify each time the victim moved, for the metal irritated the open nerve endings.

Once the victim was in place, the plaque that had proceeded him was nailed to the crossbar, which was then elevated and, with a thud, dropped into place on the pointed stake.

Before the elevation, the condemned man's arms formed a 90-degree angle with his body. After elevation, the sag caused by the weight of an average man's body decreased this angle to 65 degrees, exerting a tremendous pull on each nail.

There was no need to nail the feet, but the guards were usually irritated by the inevitable flailing. To prevent this, they put one foot over the other and drove a nail through both. But this merely prolonged death.

If the Romans didn't nail the feet, the victim's body would hang on its arms, causing it to go into a spasm that prevented exhalation. The victim soon suffocated from an inability to use his respiratory muscles. The foot nail changed this. The urge to survive is ever present, even on the cross. It didn't take long for the crucified to discover he could exhale if he lifted himself on the nail in his feet. This was intensely painful, but the desire to breathe overcame the horror of the pain. This alternating lift and drop maneuver became a reflex action after a few hours. It could prolong life for as much as two days, depending on the individual's strength and determination. To this extent, the perpetuation of his life rested in the willpower of the crucified.

As the hours wore on, the victim's mental faculties were impaired. His body became soaked with sweat. Thirst became intense. Pain and shock were tremendous. This pathetic picture continued until the victim died.

Such was the horror of the crucifixion as Jesus dragged Himself from His knees in the Garden of Gethsemane to Golgotha. He had told His disciples—and this they could understand—that a man has no greater love than to lay down his life for his friends. (See John 15:13.) Before long they'd understand a love that surpasses even this—a love so divine that He laid down His life for His enemies as well.[1]

What emotions, feelings and thoughts come to your mind as you read this account of the Crucifixion?

_____

_____

_____

_____

_____

_____

Conclude this opening section by watching the introduction to session 9 on the *Life of Jesus* DVD.

message

Read the following account of Jesus' death as told in Mark 15:33-47. As you read, keep the following questions in mind: (1) What is the significance of what Jesus says on the cross? (2) What might the disciples, Jesus' friends, and His mother, Mary, be thinking as these events unfold?

> *At the sixth hour darkness came over the whole land until the ninth hour. And at the ninth hour Jesus cried out in a loud voice, "Eloi, Eloi, lama sabachthani?"—which means, "My God, my God, why have you forsaken me?"*
>
> *When some of those standing near heard this, they said, "listen, he's calling Elijah."*

One man ran, filled a sponge with wine vinegar, put it on a stick, and offered it to Jesus to drink. "Now leave him alone. Let's see if Elijah comes to take him down," he said.

With a loud cry, Jesus breathed his last.

The curtain of the temple was torn in two from top to bottom. And when the centurion, who stood there in front of Jesus, heard his cry and saw how he died, he said, "Surely this man was the Son of God!"

Some women were watching from a distance. Among them were Mary Magdalene, Mary the mother of James the younger and of Joses, and Salome. In Galilee these women had followed him and cared for his needs. Many other women who had come up with him to Jerusalem were also there.

It was Preparation Day (that is, the day before the Sabbath). So as evening approached, Joseph of Arimathea, a prominent member of the Council, who was himself waiting for the kingdom of God, went boldly to Pilate and asked for Jesus' body. Pilate was surprised to hear that he was already dead. Summoning the centurion, he asked him if Jesus had already died. When he learned from the centurion that it was so, he gave the body to Joseph. So Joseph bought some linen cloth, took down the body, wrapped it in the linen, and placed it in a tomb cut out of rock. Then he rolled a stone against the entrance of the tomb. Mary Magdalene and Mary the mother of Joses saw where he was laid (Mark 15:33-47).

dig

1. It is incredible how God took the darkest moment in world history and turned it into the greatest demonstration of love and hope the world has ever known. According to Mark 15:34, "Jesus cried out in a loud voice, 'My God, my

God, why have you forsaken me?'" (see also Psalm 22:1).
Why do you think He said this? What did He mean by
these words?

_____

_____

_____

_____

_____

_____

_____

2. Why do you suppose the Roman centurion made the state-
    ment recorded in Mark 15:39?

_____

_____

_____

_____

_____

_____

_____

3. Using your imagination, write out a few thoughts on what
    the following people in verse 40 might have been doing or
    talking about at this time:

    Jesus' mother

_____

_____

_____

_____
_____
_____

Jesus' disciples

_____
_____
_____
_____
_____

Jesus' friends

_____
_____
_____
_____
_____

4. So, why did Christ have to die? Look at the following verses
    to discover and explore the purpose of Christ's death on
    the cross. After each section of Scripture, write down your
    understanding of why Christ had to die.

    John 3:16

    _____
    _____
    _____
    _____

Romans 5:6-8

Hebrews 9:23-29

Galatians 3:10-14

1 Peter 3:18

apply

Because Jesus Christ sacrificed His life on the cross, we have the opportunity to be set free from our sins and be called children of God. Jesus Christ had to bear the sins of the world to bridge the gap between the holiness of God and the sinfulness of humankind. There are two theological words that we use when we talk about the death of Jesus—justification and atonement.

justification

Justification means "to be made right." An easy way to remember this is to think of it as "just as if I'd never sinned." It refers to our relationship with God. Because of Christ's death, we can be made right with God.

1. Read Galatians 2:16. How do we get this justification?

_____

_____

_____

_____

_____

_____

_____

_____

_____

_____

_____

_____

2. As believers, we are justified and righteous before God not
    because of our good works but because of Christ's sacri-
    fice on the cross. Read Romans 5:1. What is the result of
    being justified in Christ?

    _____

    _____

    _____

    _____

    _____

    _____

    _____

    _____

    _____

    _____

atonement

Atonement means "to cover or pardon." This is another way of saying that our sins are forgiven. Christ paid the price of death in order for our debt of sin to be canceled. Our atonement as believers
means that our guilt and sin have been removed. Christ's death
on the cross (the shedding of blood) took the place of our spiritual death and set us free.

1. In the Old Testament, people lived under obedience to the
    Mosaic Law. Read Leviticus 17:11. How were the people to
    atone for their sins?

    _____

    _____

    _____

    _____

_____
_____
_____
_____

2. According to Leviticus 5:18, what kind of sacrifice was to be made?

_____
_____
_____
_____
_____
_____
_____
_____
_____
_____

3. The Day of Atonement was one of the major religious days of the year in Old Testament times. Read Leviticus 16:29-34. How did the Israelites celebrate this day?

_____
_____
_____
_____
_____
_____
_____
_____
_____

4. Because of Christ's death, we are no longer in bondage to the Old Testament law of atonement. His death stands as a sacrifice of atonement for all of our sins. According to 1 Peter 2:24, why did God do this?

    _____

    _____

    _____

    _____

    _____

    _____

    _____

    _____

    _____

    _____

5. Read Colossians 1:19-22. According to this passage, how does God now view us?

    _____

    _____

    _____

    _____

    _____

    _____

    _____

    _____

    _____

    _____

reflect

1. What would be different if Christ hadn't died for our sins?

    _____
    _____
    _____
    _____
    _____
    _____
    _____
    _____

2. How does it feel to know that God loved you enough to sacrifice His own Son?

    _____
    _____
    _____
    _____
    _____
    _____
    _____

3. Which of the following would be the hardest for you to sacrifice for God? Circle your top three.

friends	car	family
house	cell phone	future plans
health	talents	girlfriend/
money	music	boyfriend

4. What should our response be to God in light of His great
    love for us?

    _____

    _____

    _____

    _____

    _____

    _____

    _____

    _____

    _____

    _____

    _____

5. Is the death of Jesus a reality in your life? If so, how has it
    had an impact on you? If not, what can you do in order for
    the death of Christ to become relevant to your life?

    _____

    _____

    _____

    _____

    _____

    _____

    _____

    _____

    _____

    _____

    _____

    _____

6. What does Ephesians 2:8-9 tell us about the death of Christ?
    Why is this verse so important to remember?

_____

_____

_____

_____

_____

_____

_____

_____

_____

_____

_____

_____

_____

meditation

For God so loved the world that he gave his one
and only Son, that whoever believes in him
shall not perish but have eternal life.

JOHN 3:16

_____

Note

1. Adapted from Edward R. Bloomquist, M.D., "No Guts, No Glory," *Breakaway,* April 1992, pp.
    21-22.

session 10

the resurrection

I know that my Redeemer lives, and that in the end he will stand
upon the earth. And after my skin has been destroyed, yet in my flesh
I will see God; I myself will see him with my own eyes—I, and not another.
How my heart yearns within me!

Job 19:25-27

Life is a continuous series of unexpected surprises. You speed around town and never expect to get pulled over, but then one day a motorcycle police officer nails you with his radar gun. You are now expecting to get a ticket, but instead the officer unexpectedly lets you off with a warning.

You do your best at work, but because of the economy, you know a raise is out of the question. Then one day your boss unexpectedly informs you that you will be getting an increase in pay because of your hard work and productivity.

Little graces. The unexpected surprises that sprinkle life with spontaneity and joy. A note in the mail from a friend you haven't heard from in years. A colorful bunch of fresh cut flowers left at your door. Breakfast in bed. Little unexpected surprises remind us of God's generosity and grace. Unexpected surprises give us hope in the midst of a scary, chaotic world.

The resurrection of Jesus Christ is just the surprise we needed to bring us from sin, fear and insecurity into safety, forgiveness and wholeness before God. With more than a little grace, God showered the full extent of His love through a magnificent surprise that rocked the world. I guess you could say that the resurrection was the beginning of God's surprise party in honor of Jesus. It was a celebration filled with laughter, joy and daily surprises. And your name is on the guest list. Jesus can't wait for you to come.

As you get ready to teach this lesson, why not grab a few students and plan a surprise party for Jesus? The resurrection of Jesus is a perfect reason for a party. It will let all your teenagers know that they are welcome at a party to which they never expected to be invited.

I will never forget the day that I looked into the tomb. It changed my whole ministry. It came to me that my Savior was really alive, that His work on the cross for sinners so satisfied divine justice and divine character and divine righteousness, that I would never see my sins again. God raised Him from the dead as a guarantee to me personally that death has no more authority over the man in Christ. It has been shorn of its power . . . at the cross we see His love, but in the resurrection we see His power.

JOHN MITCHELL

the resurrection

starter

TRUE OR FALSE: Discuss if the following statements are true or false:

T   F   Every year, more than one million earthquakes shake the earth.

T   F   Elephants can spend 23 hours each day eating.

T   F   Fleas can jump up to 12 inches, 20 times their own body length.

T   F   There is an underwater hotel off the coast of Florida. Guests have to dive to the entrance.

T   F   American Roy Sullivan has been struck by lightning a record seven times.

T   F   Abraham Lincoln went to school for less than a year. He taught himself to read and write.

T   F   Sharks have no bones—a shark's skeleton is made up of cartilage.

The world can be a strange place, but even strange things can be true. All of the above statements are factual.

Now watch the introduction to session 10 on the *Life of Jesus* DVD.

message

The death of Jesus is one of the hardest stories in the Bible to read. But the good news is that the story does not end there. Our faith rests not on a weighted cross but in the empty tomb of the risen Lord.

Each of the four Gospels relates the resurrection of Jesus. As you read each of the following accounts, keep these questions in mind: (1) What is the reaction of Mary and the disciples when they discover the empty tomb? (2) What possible explanations are there for the empty tomb?

After the Sabbath, at dawn on the first day of the week, Mary Magdalene and the other Mary went to look at the tomb.

There was a violent earthquake, for an angel of the Lord came down from heaven and, going to the tomb, rolled back the stone and sat on it. His appearance was like lightning, and his clothes were white as snow. The guards were so afraid of him that they shook and became like dead men.

The angel said to the women, "Do not be afraid, for I know that you are looking for Jesus, who was crucified. He is not here; he has risen, just as he said. Come and see the place where he lay. Then go quickly and tell his disciples: 'He has risen from the dead and is going ahead of you into Galilee. There you will see him.' Now I have told you."

So the women hurried away from the tomb, afraid yet filled
with joy, and ran to tell his disciples. Suddenly Jesus met them.
"Greetings," he said. They came to him, clasped his feet and worshiped him. Then Jesus said to them, "Do not be afraid. Go and tell
my brothers to go to Galilee; there they will see me."

While the women were on their way, some of the guards went
into the city and reported to the chief priests everything that had happened. When the chief priests had met with the elders and devised a
plan, they gave the soldiers a large sum of money, telling them, "You
are to say, 'His disciples came during the night and stole him away
while we were asleep.' If this report gets to the governor, we will sat-
isfy him and keep you out of trouble." So the soldiers took the money
and did as they were instructed. And this story has been widely cir-
culated among the Jews to this very day (Matthew 28:1-15).

When the Sabbath was over, Mary Magdalene, Mary the mother
of James, and Salome bought spices so that they might go to anoint
Jesus' body. Very early on the first day of the week, just after sun-
rise, they were on their way to the tomb and they asked each other,
"Who will roll the stone away from the entrance of the tomb?"

But when they looked up, they saw that the stone, which was
very large, had been rolled away. As they entered the tomb, they
saw a young man dressed in a white robe sitting on the right side,
and they were alarmed.

"Don't be alarmed," he said. "You are looking for Jesus the
Nazarene, who was crucified. He has risen! He is not here. See the
place where they laid him. But go, tell his disciples and Peter, 'He
is going ahead of you into Galilee. There you will see him, just as
he told you.' "

Trembling and bewildered, the women went out and fled from the tomb. They said nothing to anyone, because they were afraid (Mark 16:1-8).

On the first day of the week, very early in the morning, the women took the spices they had prepared and went to the tomb. They found the stone rolled away from the tomb, but when they entered, they did not find the body of the Lord Jesus. While they were wondering about this, suddenly two men in clothes that gleamed like lightning stood beside them. In their fright the women bowed down with their faces to the ground, but the men said to them, "Why do you look for the living among the dead? He is not here; he has risen! Remember how he told you, while he was still with you in Galilee: 'The Son of Man must be delivered into the hands of sinful men, be crucified and on the third day be raised again.' " Then they remembered his words.

When they came back from the tomb, they told all these things to the Eleven and to all the others. It was Mary Magdalene, Joanna, Mary the mother of James, and the others with them who told this to the apostles. But they did not believe the women, because their words seemed to them like nonsense. Peter, however, got up and ran to the tomb. Bending over, he saw the strips of linen lying by themselves, and he went away, wondering to himself what had happened (Luke 24:1-12).

Early on the first day of the week, while it was still dark, Mary Magdalene went to the tomb and saw that the stone had been removed from the entrance. So she came running to Simon Peter

and the other disciple, the one Jesus loved, and said, "They have taken the Lord out of the tomb, and we don't know where they have put him!"

So Peter and the other disciple started for the tomb. Both were running, but the other disciple outran Peter and reached the tomb first. He bent over and looked in at the strips of linen lying there but did not go in. Then Simon Peter, who was behind him, arrived and went into the tomb. He saw the strips of linen lying there, as well as the burial cloth that had been around Jesus' head. The cloth was folded up by itself, separate from the linen. Finally the other disciple, who had reached the tomb first, also went inside. He saw and believed. (They still did not understand from Scripture that Jesus had to rise from the dead.)

Then the disciples went back to their homes, but Mary stood outside the tomb crying. As she wept, she bent over to look into the tomb and saw two angels in white, seated where Jesus' body had been, one at the head and the other at the foot.

They asked her, "Woman, why are you crying?"

"They have taken my Lord away," she said, "and I don't know where they have put him." At this, she turned around and saw Jesus standing there, but she did not realize that it was Jesus.

"Woman," he said, "why are you crying? Who is it you are looking for?"

Thinking he was the gardener, she said, "Sir, if you have carried him away, tell me where you have put him, and I will get him."

Jesus said to her, "Mary."

She turned toward him and cried out in Aramaic, "Rabboni!" (which means Teacher).

Jesus said, "Do not hold on to me, for I have not yet returned to the Father. Go instead to my brothers and tell them, 'I am returning to my Father and your Father, to my God and your God.'"

Mary Magdalene went to the disciples with the news: "I have seen the Lord!" And she told them that he had said these things to her (John 20:1-18).

dig

In order to believe in the resurrection of Jesus, you need not commit intellectual suicide. There are actually a number of facts that are unexplainable if Jesus did not actually rise from the dead. Let's explore these facts.

Jesus foretold His resurrection
Read Matthew 16:21 and Matthew 17:22-23. Why were the disciples distressed by the words of Jesus?

_____

_____

_____

_____

_____

_____

_____

If Jesus did not rise from the dead on the third day, these verses from Matthew would make Him out to be a liar!

the disciples were transformed
The testimony of eyewitnesses and the transformation of the disciples can only logically be explained by the resurrection appearances of Jesus.

1. At the crucifixion, the followers of Jesus were in despair.
   Their hopes for a Messiah had been crushed. Yet after three
   days, their lives were transformed. Read 1 Corinthians
   15:3-8. List those to whom Jesus appeared after He was
   raised from the dead.

   _____

   _____

   _____

   _____

   _____

   _____

   _____

   _____

   _____

   _____

2. Peter is one example of the life-changing impact that the
   resurrection had on the disciples. Read Matthew 26:69-75.
   What had Peter done just a few days before?

   _____

   _____

   _____

   _____

   _____

   _____

   _____

   _____

   _____

   _____

3. As recorded in Acts 2:14-37, what did Peter proclaim after the resurrection of Jesus?

_____

_____

_____

_____

_____

_____

_____

_____

_____

the resurrection is the only explanation
for the empty tomb

Many people throughout history have tried to disprove the resurrection, for it is true that if the resurrection of Jesus can be disproved, the cornerstone of the Christian faith would be destroyed.

1. According to Paul in 1 Corinthians 15:17-19, why is the resurrection so important?

_____

_____

_____

_____

_____

_____

_____

_____

2. What were the precautions taken, both by the friends of
    Jesus and by His enemies, to ensure that His body would
    not be stolen?

    His friends (see Mark 15:6)

    _____

    _____

    _____

    _____

    _____

    His enemies (see Matthew 27:62-66)

    _____

    _____

    _____

    _____

    _____

3. Listed below are the most common theories that skeptics
    have used to refute the resurrection. Using the Scriptures
    you have looked at in this session so far, show the fallacy
    of these theories.

    THEORY   REFUTED BY . . .

    The disciples stole and hid
    the body.   _____

    The Roman or Jewish author-
    ities took the body.   _____

    Jesus never died. He walked
    out of the tomb.   _____

THEORY	REFUTED BY . . .
The women and disciples went to the wrong tomb.	
The disciples were hallucinating and didn't really witness Jesus' resurrection.	

the resurrection is the reason for the beginning of the church

The resurrection is the reason for the beginning of the Christian Church and its rapid growth. Within a short period of time, the Christian faith spread all over the Roman Empire and beyond. The disciples always spoke of the resurrected and living Christ.

1. What was the main subject of Peter's sermon found in Acts 2:29-32?

2. What was the response of Peter's audience, according to Acts 2:37-42?

_____

_____

_____

apply

1. Jesus tried countless times throughout His life to prepare
    the disciples for His crucifixion and the resurrection. Why
    do you think the disciples just didn't get it until it was ac-
    tually happening?

_____

_____

_____

_____

_____

_____

_____

2. If you were one of the first people to visit the tomb after
    Jesus' death, what would have been your thoughts and
    feelings at seeing the empty tomb?

_____

_____

_____

_____

_____

_____

3. After Jesus' resurrection, He appeared to several people individually or in groups. Jesus appeared to Mary in her sorrow (see John 20:10-18). What pain in your life do you need Jesus to come and soothe?

_____

_____

_____

_____

_____

_____

_____

_____

_____

_____

4. Jesus appeared to the disciples in their fear (see John 20:19-23). For what fears can Jesus give you confidence?

_____

_____

_____

_____

_____

_____

_____

_____

_____

_____

_____

5. Jesus appeared to Peter after his denial (see John 21:15-19;
   see also John 18:15-18,25-27). In what ways have you "de-
   nied" Christ? Have you asked for Jesus' forgiveness?

_____

_____

_____

_____

_____

_____

_____

_____

_____

_____

6. Jesus appeared to Thomas in his doubts (see John 20:24-
   29). What doubts or questions do you have that you need
   Christ to answer?

_____

_____

_____

_____

_____

_____

_____

_____

_____

_____

reflect

The resurrection of Jesus Christ is the most important event in human history. This single miracle has transformed our world like no other. The Christian faith rests on the fact that Jesus Christ actually rose from the dead. Based on this knowledge, we can be assured of the following: (1) All that He claimed about Himself must be true, (2) all that He said about life must be true, (3) our sins are truly forgiven, and (4) Christians have eternal life and will be resurrected from the dead just as Christ was.

1. How should the fact that Jesus *said* He would rise on the third day and actually *did* impact our faith?

   _____

   _____

   _____

   _____

   _____

   _____

   _____

   _____

2. How does the resurrection of Jesus separate Christianity from other religions?

   _____

   _____

   _____

   _____

_____

_____

_____

_____

3. Why do some people still deny Christianity even after hearing of the resurrection?

    _____

    _____

    _____

    _____

    _____

    _____

    _____

    _____

    _____

4. Are there parts of the resurrection that are hard for you to believe? Write your thoughts below.

    _____

    _____

    _____

    _____

    _____

    _____

    _____

    _____

    _____

5. The resurrection means that if you believe, you are for-
    given of your sins and made right with God. How can you
    live a life that claims and reflects this truth?

_____

_____

_____

_____

_____

_____

_____

_____

_____

_____

_____

meditation

Jesus said to her, "I am the resurrection and the life. He who
believes in me will live, even though he dies; and whoever
lives and believes in me will never die."

JOHN 11:25-26

the ascension of Jesus

Let us not become weary in doing good, for at the proper time we will reap a harvest if we do not give up. Therefore, as we have opportunity, let us do good to all people, especially to those who belong to the family of believers.

GALATIANS 6:9-10

I am grateful for the family in which I grew up. Like any other family, mine was not perfect. The Cleavers we were not, but we were a good family. My mom and dad had seven screaming, rambunctious children, and I was number five. Two boys . . . five girls. My brother, Neil, and I were definitely outnumbered.

Growing up, we all had our fair share of fights and arguments. Yet despite all this, we were still a good family. My parents never were separated or divorced. In fact, many of the values and character qualities that I learned from my folks are the same things I've taught my two girls.

When I think about the home environment I grew up in and then contrast it with the home lives of many of the students I've worked with, I am amazed at God's blessing in my life. There are so many young people today whose anger, bitterness and rebellion from God are rooted in what is happening at home. When you look at the students in your ministry who have troubled home lives, don't you just wish you could give them warm and secure homes to live in? How many problems and struggles could be prevented if these students lived in homes filled with love?

Short of taking legal action, you and I both know that it's almost impossible to shield our students from the damage done in abusive homes. The one hope—the most valuable gift we can give them—is the promises of Jesus found in this lesson. Jesus' ascension and the promise of His abiding presence in our lives can give students a firm foundation for their lives. Jesus' presence and the extended family of God can give them the warm sense of security, comfort and community that they don't find at home. You have the remarkable opportunity to show teenagers how to belong to and create loving families of their own someday.

The power of the Resurrection is the power of personal regeneration.
Resurrection always spells regeneration. The two things must always be
kept together: the new world and the new person. Resurrection is not
just a passport to heaven, but a power to change us now.

LLOYD OGILVIE

the ascension of Jesus

starter

YOUR LEGACY: The word "legacy" means "money or property left to someone in a will," but today we often use the word to signify how an individual will be remembered. What legacy do you want to leave behind? What legacy are you already leaving? What do you want to be remembered for?

I want to be remembered as a Christian man who loved people, made people laugh, & enjoyed life

I am currently thought of as a person who is goofy & wants to serve God

I want to be remembered as a person who cared about others, and helped others, and was humble.

What three words or phrases would you want to be used to describe your life at your funeral?

1. _Jesus Follower_
2. _Loved to Enjoy Life_
3. _That'll Learn 'Em_

Now watch the introduction to session 11 on the *Life of Jesus* DVD.

message

→ (Rose from the dead)

After His resurrection, Jesus appeared to His followers during the next 40 days before His ascension—or "rising upwards"—into heaven. Read the following passage from Acts 1:1-11. As you read, keep in mind the following questions: (1) What might the disciples have been thinking during the ascension? (2) Why didn't Jesus just remain on earth after His resurrection?

→ Remember ~ This Really Happened. This is as real as 9/11
Do you all Remember 9/11

> *In my former book, Theophilus, I wrote about all that Jesus began to do and to teach until the day he was taken up to heaven, after giving instructions through the Holy Spirit to the apostles he had chosen. After his suffering, he showed himself to these men and gave many convincing proofs that he was alive. He appeared to them over a period of forty days and spoke about the kingdom of God. On one occasion, while he was eating with them, he gave them this command: "Do not leave Jerusalem, but wait for the gift my Father promised, which you have heard me speak about. For John baptized with water, but in a few days you will be baptized with the Holy Spirit."*
>
> *So when they met together, they asked him, "Lord, are you at this time going to restore the kingdom to Israel?"*

He said to them: "It is not for you to know the times or dates the Father has set by his own authority. But you will receive power when the Holy Spirit comes on you; and you will be my witnesses in Jerusalem, and in all Judea and Samaria, and to the ends of the earth."

After he said this, he was taken up before their very eyes, and a cloud hid him from their sight.

They were looking intently up into the sky as he was going, when suddenly two men dressed in white stood beside them. "Men of Galilee," they said, "why do you stand here looking into the sky? This same Jesus, who has been taken from you into heaven, will come back in the same way you have seen him go into heaven" (Acts 1:1-11).

These verses are actual historical occurences
If not for Jesus com; dig back from the dead
after crucified, we would not be here in this

1. How does the disciples' statement, "Lord, are you at this *building* time going to restore the kingdom to Israel?" demonstrate that the disciples still did not fully understand the com- *to do* plete role of Jesus Christ? (Remember that at this time, the *today* Jews were under Roman domination and believed that Jesus would bring political independence to the Jews and restore the nation of Israel.)

_____

They thought of an earthly kingdom
+ Jesus setting up heavenly kingdom
a Church

_____

_____

_____

2. Although Jesus leaves the disciples, He tells them that God will send the Holy Spirit. According to the following verses, what is the role of the Holy Spirit?

John 14:26

Will teach them & remind them of what Jesus taught the

John 16:7-8

Jesus says once he leaves, Holy Spirit will come and help them

Acts 9:31

Holy Spirit encourages Christians

1 Corinthians 6:19

Holy Spirit

Body is temple of holy spirit, received from God

3. What event is foretold in verse 11 of the passage in Acts?

   The return of Jesus

4. According to Mark 16:19, where did Christ go after the ascension?

   Back to Heaven, & sat at the right hand of God

5. According to the following verses, what is Christ doing in heaven?

   John 14:1-3

   Preparing a place for his Apostles & us

Romans 8:34

He is interceding for us. When we pray to God Jesus is telling God our prayers. He is our friend. When we die & go to heaven (if we are a Christian), He will tell God we are his & we will be with him

apply *eternally*

The disciples had seen Jesus work miracles. They had observed the agony of His death and the joy and confusion of His resurrection. Now, after 40 days on earth in His resurrected body, Jesus had ascended into heaven, where He would sit at the right hand of God. The disciples had watched, amazed and stunned, as He disappeared into the sky. After the ascension, the disciples were transformed people. Our response in the twenty-first century should be the same response as the disciples had back in the first century.

joy and worship

1. Read Luke 24:50-53. What was the response of the disciples after Jesus ascended into heaven?

They had great Joy

10 days later they had the day of Pentecost. People from all over the world were gathered for that Jewish feast

Peter preached to all of them & read what happened in Acts 2:38.

↳ Church was started on this day

↳ & the rest is history

Jesus & God alive then and still alive today

2. Imagine you are a disciple. How would you have felt if you had just witnessed Jesus rising up into heaven?

_____

_____

_____

_____

_____

_____

_____

_____

_____

_____

_____

3. Are joy and worship in the Lord a central part of your spiritual life? If not, what steps can you take to make these elements a greater portion of your life?

_____

_____

_____

_____

_____

_____

_____

_____

_____

_____

_____

_____

power

1. What kind of power is Jesus talking about in Acts 1:8?

2. What kind of help does the Holy Spirit provide to us?

3. Do you find it easy or hard to call on the Holy Spirit for guidance and support? Why?

_____
_____
_____
_____

4. God promises that all things are possible through Him
    (see Philippians 4:13). What difficulties are you facing
    that you need to rely on the aid of the Holy Spirit to guide
    you through?

_____
_____
_____
_____
_____
_____
_____
_____

proclamation

1. According to Mark 16:19-20, what did the disciples do
    when Jesus was taken up to heaven?

_____
_____
_____
_____
_____
_____
_____

2. The word "proclaim" means to announce, tell or preach. The disciples proclaimed to people everywhere the resurrection and the new life available in Jesus. Of course, proclaiming truth can have consequences. What might have been some of the consequences for the disciples—or for us today—of proclaiming the risen Jesus?

3. What would have happened if the disciples had not fervently and passionately gone out into the world and proclaimed the good news of Jesus?

4. How are you proclaiming Christ in your own life? What things can you do to proclaim Him more?

_____

_____

_____

_____

_____

_____

_____

_____

_____

_____

reflect

1. Why do you think Jesus ascended into heaven? Why not just stay on earth?

_____

_____

_____

_____

_____

_____

_____

_____

2. The disciples had the opportunity to walk and talk with Jesus. If you had that same opportunity today, what would
   you ask? What would you want to know or understand?

   _____

   _____

   _____

   _____

   _____

   _____

   _____

3. Although you may not have witnessed a miracle, describe
   a time when you witnessed the hand of God on your life.

   _____

   _____

   _____

   _____

   _____

   _____

   _____

4. How did this experience affect your faith?

   _____

   _____

   _____

   _____

_____

_____

_____

_____

_____

5. Who do you know who needs the good news of Jesus Christ
    proclaimed to them?

_____

_____

_____

_____

_____

_____

_____

_____

6. What fears hinder you from proclaiming Jesus to those in
    your life who do not know Him?

_____

_____

_____

_____

_____

_____

_____

7. In Acts 1:7, Jesus says, "It is not for you to know the times or dates the Father has set by his own authority." What does this mean? How can we apply these words to our own lives?

_____

_____

_____

_____

_____

_____

_____

_____

_____

meditation

Let us run with perseverance the race marked out for us.
Let us fix our eyes on Jesus, the author and perfecter of our
faith, who for the joy set before him endured the cross, scorn-
ing its shame, and sat down at the right hand of the throne of
God. Consider him who endured such opposition from sinful
men, so that you will not grow weary and lose heart.

HEBREWS 12:1-3

the second coming

He who testifies to these things says, "Yes, I am coming soon." Amen.
Come, Lord Jesus. The grace of the Lord Jesus be with God's people. Amen.
REVELATION 22:20-21

A few years ago, I attended a youth worker's conference in which a fellow youth worker shared with me a simple list of qualities he looked for in students who wanted to serve on his student ministry team. He looked for students who were faithful, available and teachable. Ever since that conversation years ago, I've used that same list of character qualities to disciple and develop students on my student ministry team. I also use these qualities as a filter in my own life to make sure I'm growing in my relationship with God.

When we study the second coming of Christ, only by being faithful to God will we be ready for Jesus' return. If we make ourselves available to the Holy Spirit every day, we will be prepared to meet Jesus with eager anticipation. If we remain teachable and with open hearts ready to receive God's correction and instruction, we will remind ourselves of our temporary residence here on planet Earth.

Whether you are a full-time, a part-time or a volunteer youth worker, God isn't only interested in seeing these qualities developed in students' lives. He wants you to be *faithful*. He wants you to be *available*. And He wants you to be *teachable*. The same qualities we desire to develop in the lives of teenagers are the very same ones God wants to create in our lives.

As youth workers, we are co-learners, co-followers and also co-disciples with our students. The only thing that separates us from them is age and experience. We all follow the same Lord. Each one of us must individually prepare for the return of Christ. Staying faithful, available and teachable will keep our eyes on the sky and not on earth.

Because we do not know the day or the hour of our Lord's return,
we must constantly be ready. The believer who starts to neglect the
"blessed hope" (Titus 2:13) will gradually develop a cold heart, a worldly
attitude, and an unfaithful life (Luke 12:35-48).
WARREN WIERSBE

the second coming

starter

INSIDER TIP: Imagine that you have received a special insider tip from heaven that Jesus will return in 10 years. What would you do with that information? Who would you tell? What would you do differently with your life? With your time?

_____

_____

_____

_____

_____

_____

_____

_____

_____

_____

_____

_____

How would your response be different if you knew that Jesus would return in 100 years? In one year?

_____

_____

_____

_____

_____

_____

_____

_____

If Jesus returned tomorrow, would you have any regrets? Would you have any longings for one more day to make things right with someone, to make the right decision, to make more of a difference? What change can you make today to live a life prepared for Christ's return?

_____

_____

_____

_____

_____

_____

_____

_____

Now watch the introduction to session 12 on the _Life of Jesus_ DVD.

message

From Jesus' ascension to today, people have tried to predict when Jesus' second coming will take place. Jesus Himself spoke very little about the end times; however, His words in Matthew 24:1-31 are one of those rare exceptions. In this passage, the disciples ask Jesus to tell them when and what to expect in the last days. As you read Jesus' response, consider these questions: (1) How does Jesus describe the end times? (2) What kinds of events does Jesus warn are *not* signs of the end times?

> *Jesus left the temple and was walking away when his disciples came up to him to call his attention to its buildings. "Do you see all these things?" he asked. "I tell you the truth, not one stone here will be left on another; every one will be thrown down."*
>
> *As Jesus was sitting on the Mount of Olives, the disciples came to him privately. "Tell us," they said, "when will this happen, and what will be the sign of your coming and of the end of the age?"*
>
> *Jesus answered: "Watch out that no one deceives you. For many will come in my name, claiming, 'I am the Christ,' and will deceive many. You will hear of wars and rumors of wars, but see to it that you are not alarmed. Such things must happen, but the end is still to come. Nation will rise against nation, and kingdom against kingdom. There will be famines and earthquakes in various places. All these are the beginning of birth pains.*
>
> *"Then you will be handed over to be persecuted and put to death, and you will be hated by all nations because of me. At that time many will turn away from the faith and will betray and hate each other, and many false prophets will appear and deceive many people. Because of the increase of wickedness, the love of most will grow cold, but he who stands firm to the end will be saved. And this*

gospel of the kingdom will be preached in the whole world as a testimony to all nations, and then the end will come.

"So when you see standing in the holy place 'the abomination that causes desolation,' spoken of through the prophet Daniel—let the reader understand—then let those who are in Judea flee to the mountains. Let no one on the roof of his house go down to take anything out of the house. Let no one in the field go back to get his cloak. How dreadful it will be in those days for pregnant women and nursing mothers! Pray that your flight will not take place in winter or on the Sabbath. For then there will be great distress, unequaled from the beginning of the world until now—and never to be equaled again. If those days had not been cut short, no one would survive, but for the sake of the elect those days will be shortened. At that time if anyone says to you, 'Look, here is the Christ!' or 'There he is!' do not believe it. For false Christs and false prophets will appear and perform great signs and miracles to deceive even the elect—if that were possible. See, I have told you ahead of time.

"So if anyone tells you, 'There he is, out in the desert,' do not go out; or 'Here he is, in the inner rooms,' do not believe it. For as lightning that comes from the east and is visible even in the west, so will be the coming of the Son of Man. Wherever there is a carcass, there the vultures will gather.

Immediately after the distress of those days, 'the sun will be darkened, and the moon will not give its light; the stars will fall from the sky, and the heavenly bodies will be shaken.'

"At that time the sign of the Son of Man will appear in the sky, and all the nations of the earth will mourn. They will see the Son of Man coming on the clouds of the sky, with power and great glory. And he will send his angels with a loud trumpet call, and they will gather his elect from the four winds, from one end of the heavens to the other" (Matthew 24:1-31).

dig

This great passage of Scripture focuses on the teachings of Jesus concerning the destruction of Jerusalem and His second coming. Jesus' words remind us that the true issue is not the "hows" or "whens" of the second coming, but rather in learning to live in the present in the light of the future events.[1]

1. Throughout history people have set dates for Christ's return and been mistaken. What events did Jesus warn the disciples might deceive them into thinking the end was at hand?

_____

_____

_____

_____

_____

_____

_____

_____

2. Before the end comes, what dangers will believers face, and how are we to handle them?

_____

_____

_____

_____

_____

_____

_____

3. How will we be able to distinguish the false Christ from
    the true Christ?

    _____

    _____

    _____

    _____

    _____

    _____

    _____

    _____

4. Read Matthew 24:32-51. What do these verses say about
    the timing of Christ's return?

    _____

    _____

    _____

    _____

    _____

    _____

    _____

    _____

    _____

apply

This important teaching of Jesus helps us look at His second coming in the light of three key words: (1) preparedness, (2) watchfulness and (3) faithfulness. You may not be able to figure out all that

you would like to know about Christ's return, but these are steps you can take to prepare for it.

preparedness

1. How do the parables of the thief and the wise and wicked servants (see Matthew 24:42-51) emphasize the importance of living in the light of Christ's return?

_____

_____

_____

_____

_____

_____

_____

_____

_____

_____

2. Why should we prepare *now* for Christ's return?

_____

_____

_____

_____

_____

_____

_____

_____

_____

_____

3. What does being prepared for Christ's coming actually
    mean to you?

    _____

    _____

    _____

    _____

    _____

    _____

    _____

    _____

    _____

4. The following passages describe six ways to prepare for
    the second coming of Christ. Share what each verse re-
    veals about how we can prepare for His return.

    Proverbs 3:5-6

    _____

    _____

    _____

    _____

    _____

    Isaiah 40:29-31

    _____

    _____

    _____

    _____

    _____

Micah 6:8

_____

_____

_____

_____

_____

Matthew 16:24

_____

_____

_____

_____

_____

Luke 10:27

_____

_____

_____

_____

_____

Romans 12:1-2

_____

_____

_____

_____

_____

watchfulness

Theologian William Barclay once noted the following about being watchful: "To live without watchfulness invites disaster. A thief does not send a letter saying when he is going to burgle a house; his principal weapon in his nefarious undertakings is surprise; therefore a householder who has valuables in his house must maintain a constant guard. But to get this picture right, we must remember that the watchdog of the Christian for the coming of Christ is not that of terror-stricken fear and shivering apprehension: it is the watching of eager expectation for the coming of glory and joy."[2]

1. What does it mean in practical terms to have an attitude of watchfulness?

    _____

    _____

    _____

    _____

    _____

    _____

    _____

    _____

2. Read 1 Thessalonians 5:1-11. What advice does Paul give Christians on how to be watchful for the coming of Christ?

    _____

    _____

    _____

    _____

    _____

    _____

    _____

3. Are you living a life that is prepared and watchful for the
    second coming? If not, what do you need to change?

    _____

    _____

    _____

    _____

    _____

    _____

    _____

faithfulness

Faithfulness is one of the key ingredients in living a consistent
Christian life. The Scripture tells us that the rewards of faithfulness are great.

1. Read Matthew 24:45-51. What is the reward for the fol-
    lowing servants in this parable?

    The faithful servant

    _____

    _____

    _____

    _____

    The unfaithful servant

    _____

    _____

    _____

    _____

2. What does "being faithful" really mean?

    _____

    _____

    _____

    _____

    _____

    _____

3. On the scale below, how would you rank your general level
    of faithfulness to God?

1	2	3	4	5	6	7	8	9	10

    Never   Sometimes   Always
    faithful   faithful   faithful

4. In what areas is it easiest for you to be faithful? In what ar-
    eas is it hardest?

    _____

    _____

    _____

    _____

    _____

    _____

    _____

reflect

1. How do you view the second coming of Jesus Christ? With
    fear? With excitement? With doubt? With indifference?

With hope? What are your greatest fears about the future?

_____

_____

_____

_____

_____

_____

_____

2. Why is there so much interest in the second coming?

_____

_____

_____

_____

_____

_____

_____

_____

3. What changes can you make to be more prepared, more watchful and more faithful for Jesus' second coming?

_____

_____

_____

_____

_____

_____

_____

4. Do you think the world is ready for Jesus' return? Why or why not?

_____

_____

_____

_____

_____

_____

_____

_____

_____

_____

meditation

Heaven and earth will pass away,
but my words will never pass away.

MATTHEW 24:35

Notes

1. Some of the questions in this section are adapted from an excellent workbook by Stephen and Jacalyn Eyre, *Matthew: Being Discipled by Jesus* (Downers Grove, IL: InterVarsity Press, 1987), pp. 65-66.
2. William Barclay, *The Gospel of Matthew, Vol. II, The Daily Study Bible Series* (Philadelphia, PA: Westminster Press, 1975), p. 317.

HOME WORD

WHERE PARENTS GET REAL ANSWERS

Get Equipped with HomeWord...

LISTEN
HomeWord Radio
programs reach over 800 communities nationwide with *HomeWord with Jim Burns* – a daily ½ hour interview feature, *HomeWord Snapshots* – a daily 1 minute family drama, and *HomeWord this Week* – a ½ hour weekend edition of the daily program, and our one-hour program.

CLICK
HomeWord.com
provides advice and resources to millions of visitors each year. A truly interactive website, HomeWord.com provides access to parent newsletter, Q&As, online broadcasts, tip sheets, our online store and more.

READ
HomeWord Resources
parent newsletters, equip families and Churches worldwide with practical Q&As, online broadcasts, tip sheets, our online store and more. Many of these resources are also packaged digitally to meet the needs of today's busy parents.

ATTEND
HomeWord Events
Understanding Your Teenager, Building Healthy Morals & Values, Generation 2 Generation and Refreshing Your Marriage are held in over 100 communities nationwide each year. HomeWord events educate and encourage parents while providing answers to life's most pressing parenting and family questions.

A
Ministry *Jim Burns*
with

In response to the overwhelming needs of parents and families, Jim Burns founded HomeWord in 1985. HomeWord, a Christian organization, equips and encourages parents, families, and churches worldwide.

Find Out More
Sign up for our FREE daily
e-devotional and parent e-newsletter
at HomeWord.com, or call 800.397.9725.

HomeWord.com

Small Group Curriculum Kits

Confident Parenting Kit

This is a must-have resource for today's family! Let Jim Burns help you to tackle overcrowded lives, negative family patterns, while creating a grace-filled home and raising kids who love God and themselves.

Kit contains:
- 6 sessions on DVD featuring Dr. Jim Burns
- CD with reproducible small group leader's guide and participant guides
- poster, bulletin insert, and more

Creating an Intimate Marriage Kit

Dr. Jim Burns wants every couple to experience a marriage filled with A.W.E.: affection, warmth, and encouragement. He shows husbands and wives how to make their marriage a priority as they discover ways to repair the past, communicate and resolve conflict, refresh their marriage spiritually, and more!

Kit contains:
- 6 sessions on DVD featuring Dr. Jim Burns
- CD with reproducible small group leader's guide and participant guides
- poster, bulletin insert, and more

Parenting Teenagers for Positive Results

This popular resource is designed for small groups and Sunday schools. The DVD features real family situations played out in humorous family vignettes followed by words of wisdom by youth and family expert, Jim Burns, Ph.D.

Kit contains:
- 6 sessions on DVD featuring Dr. Jim Burns
- CD with reproducible small group leader's guide and participant guides
- poster, bulletin insert, and more

Teaching Your Children Healthy Sexuality Kit

Trusted family authority Dr. Jim Burns outlines a simple and practical guide for parents on how to develop in their children a healthy perspective regarding their bodies and sexuality. Promotes godly values about sex and relationships.

Kit contains:
- 6 sessions on DVD featuring Dr. Jim Burns
- CD with reproducible small group leader's guide and participant guides
- poster, bulletin insert, and more

Tons of helpful resources for youth workers, parents and youth. Visit our online store at www.HomeWord.com or call us at 800-397-9725

Parent and Family Resources from HomeWord for you and your kids...

One Life Kit

Your kids only have one life – help them discover the greatest adventure life has to offer! 50 fresh devotional readings that cover many of the major issues of life and faith your kids are wrestling with such as sex, family relationships, trusting God, worry, fatigue and daily surrender. And it's perfect for you and your kids to do together!

Addicted to God Kit

Is your kids' time absorbed by MySpace, text messaging and hanging out at the mall? This devotional will challenge them to adopt thankfulness, make the most of their days and never settle for mediocrity! Fifty days in the Scripture is bound to change your kids' lives forever.

Devotions on the Run Kit

These devotionals are short, simple, and spiritual. They will encourage you to take action in your walk with God. Each study stays in your heart throughout the day, providing direction and clarity when it is most needed.

90 Days Through the New Testament Kit

Downloadable devotional. Author Jim Burns put together a Bible study devotional program for himself to follow, one that would take him through the New Testament in three months. His simple plan was so powerful that he was called to share it with others. A top seller!

Small Group Curriculum Kits

Confirming Your Faith Kit

Rite-of-Passage curriculum empowers youth to make wise decisions...to choose Christ. Help them take ownership of their faith! Lead them to do this by experiencing a vital Christian lifestyle.

Kit contains:
- 13 engaging lessons
- Ideas for retreats and special Celebration
- Solid foundational Bible concepts
- 1 leaders guide and 6 student journals (booklets)

10 Building Blocks Kit

Learn to live, laugh, love, and play together as a family. When you learn the 10 essential principles for creating a happy, close-knit household, you'll discover a family that shines with love for God and one another! Use this curriculum to help equip families in your church.

Kit contains:
- 10 sessions on DVD featuring Dr. Jim Burns
- CD with reproducible small group leader's guide and participant guides
- poster and bulletin insert
- 10 Building Blocks book

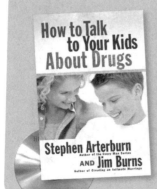

How to Talk to Your Kids About Drugs Kit

Dr. Jim Burns speaks to parents about the important topic of talking to their kids about drugs. You'll find everything you need to help parents learn and implement a plan for drug-proofing their kids.

Kit contains:
- 2 session DVD featuring family expert Dr. Jim Burns
- CD with reproducible small group leader's guide and participant guides
- poster, bulletin insert, and more
- How to Talk to Your Kids About Drugs book

Tons of helpful resources for youth workers, parents and youth. Visit our online store at www.HomeWord.com or call us at 800-397-9725